I SPEAK OF AFRICA

THE STORY OF
LONDOLOZI GAME RESERVE
1926 — 1996

LONDOLOZI GAME RESERVE
A MEMBER OF CONSERVATION CORPORATION AFRICA

This book is dedicated to Madeleine Varty,
the mother of Londolozi.

I SPEAK OF AFRICA

THE STORY OF LONDOLOZI GAME RESERVE
1926 — 1996

Directed by
SHAN VARTY

Written by
MOLLY BUCHANAN

Photography
LEX HES, PETER JOHNSON AND GUY STUBBS

Design and illustrations
JOHAN HOEKSTRA

**LONDOLOZI
PUBLISHERS**

South African Library Cataloguing
in Publication Data
VARTY, Shan 1956 –
BUCHANAN, Molly 1934 –
I SPEAK OF AFRICA
1. Game reserves

Reproduction by Beith Digital
South Africa
Typesetting: Molly Buchanan
Printing: Tien Wah Press
Singapore

ISBN 0-620-20646-2

First edition, first impression 1997
Published by Londolozi Publishers
P.O. Box 4752
Rivonia 2128
South Africa

I speak of Africa and golden joys.
— *William Shakespeare*

FOREWORD

Tourism forms a vital part of our strategy for sustained economic growth and development. But within the industry competition is stiff. We are one of many countries in Africa that has beautiful and impressive places and we must therefore adopt a professional approach, upgrade our skills and market ourselves aggressively.

One of our most progressive parks is Londolozi Game Reserve. They have taken the initiative to restore the habitat with the result that wildlife has flourished not only on their own land but also through the surrounding reserves.

During my long walk to freedom, I had the rare privilege to visit Londolozi. There I saw people of all races living in harmony amidst the beauty that mother nature offers. There I saw a living lion in the wild.

Londolozi represents a model of the dream I cherish for the future of nature preservation in our country.

Mandela

Nelson Mandela

Opposite: John Varty, President Nelson Mandela, Dave and Shan Varty.

GLOSSARY OF SOUTH AFRICAN WORDS

Boma   An enclosure with a palisade or fence of thorn bush set up to protect cattle.

Donga   A gulley created by soil erosion.

Dambo   The system of drainage lines from vlei or marsh.

Kloof   A gorge in a mountain range.

Kraal   A cattle enclosure or a hut village.

Nkosi   Zulu for king.

Rondavel   A thatched, circular building.

Seepline   A spongy area of clay soils which hold moisture, retarding the growth of trees but encouraging grass.

Spoor   The track left by an animal.

Ubuntu   Humane, kind, thoughtful of others.

Vlei   Marshy ground that usually feeds a stream.

CONTENTS

INTRODUCTION

"I SPEAK OF AFRICA" is in part a story of the birth of the Londolozi Game Reserve and the record of 70 years spanning four generations of a family history in Africa. It also embodies a hope that the people of the world will discover that if they are to enjoy a quality of life and the beauty of our planet they must reach out for a new order; turning their considerable energies and talents towards restoring and reinstating the laws of nature.

The world has slowly emerged from the plundering mentality which reached its zenith at the turn of the century and is developing a realisation for the need to conserve and protect. Londolozi, where habitat was destroyed unthinkingly by man over the first 75 years of this century, represents in microcosm what is happening all over the world. This book also reflects on our options for a future which no longer permits the wanton destruction of the earth's resources in the name of development and profit.

As we enter the new millennium, the holders of the world's investment capital are the people to whom we must look to lead the charge to restore the integrity of the planet's 'grand design'. I believe that the implementation of dramatic global restoration projects and the management of environmental degradation will represent the next great challenge for the world's business and political leaders.

The story of Londolozi Game Reserve and the birth of Conservation Corporation represents one small step in this new and exciting future. I hope it will inspire you to add your voice to the growing world consciousness in deciding our own destiny.

David Varty

APPRECIATION

**L**ONDOLOZI IS A STORY of the pioneering spirit of the past, of a conservation ethic and initiative that was to become a realised dream, and of people who are bonded by a common love of the wilderness. It is a story bigger than any one individual.

Pioneering men like Charles Boyd Varty and Frank Unger and their courageous wives and families explored the bushveld. These men were visionaries, way ahead of their time. Charles's son, Boyd and his wife Madeleine continued the tradition of hunting trips every July, taking their children, Claudia, John and David, to the farm Sparta when they were only a few months old. After Boyd died in 1969, Madeleine did not set foot on her adored Sparta for years. There were too many happy memories and too much heartbreak.

The book is also a record of our appreciation to all those people who over the years contributed towards the development of a magical place called Londolozi. There are many people who have played an important part in our story and whose lives became closely linked with ours. In particular Dave, John and I would like to thank Allan Taylor, Frank Unger's grandson, who inherited half of Sparta from his mother Betty Taylor, and has been a wonderful partner and a key participator in Londolozi; Luke Bailes, neighbour and friend, and the Wilkens's family who own the farm Dudley and who have been associated with the Varty's since 1932. We are deeply grateful to the many rangers and camp staff both from the old days and right up to the present time and to our visitors, many of whom became friends, who have supported us through thick and thin, returning to Londolozi again and again. On pages 210 and 211 we have included a roll of honour, naming many of those people who have given so much to Londolozi, and we hope, through the experience, have enriched their lives.

I am particularly indebted to Madeleine Varty. Without her love and commitment to Sparta there would have been no Londolozi and no story to tell. Extensive use has been made of her Sparta Game Book, in which she kept a record of the hunting expeditions from 1942 until 1969, and her historical account of the Sabi Sand Wildtuin, a private game reserve formed by the owners of the farms in the wedge of land between the Sabie and Sand rivers. This booklet was written in 1976 to commemorate the 50th anniversary of the first Sparta camp which she described as, "the seed from which the Sabi Sand grew".

It is fitting to pay tribute to the past and present owners of the Sabi Sand Wildtuin who for so many years have stood together united in the preservation and conservation of this unique habitat. The commercial operations within the Sabi Sand, including Londolozi, are totally dependent on the ongoing goodwill of the owners in maintaining the integrity of the reserve.

I would also like to thank Dave, my husband, partner and friend, who has

given me so much encouragement and support in the creation of this book and our children, Bronwyn and Boyd who are wise beyond their years, and have given me a great sense of confidence in the future. John's perceptions of future trends and his deep insight into African conservation as well as the use of his unfinished manuscript, have been of great assistance as has been the kind help and photographs provided by Gillian van Houten.

To my family and friends who said I could do it, thank you for your support. I also thank the team who made it happen. My admiration and deep gratitude goes to Molly Buchanan for her never-ending energy, passion, drive, talent and professionalism which have played a major part in recording the 70 years of Londolozi's history and to Johan Hoekstra, whose sense of style and design I believe are amongst the best in the world. In producing the book we are grateful to Harold Fridjhon and Lynn Payne for editing and proofreading, to Lex Hes, Peter Johnson (Corbis Media), Guy Stubbs, Richard du Toit, James Marshall, Mike Myers and Dupe du Plessis for their beautiful photographs, to Judith Campbell for graphic illustrations, to Steve Reynolds and Paddy Hagelthorn for the use of their butterfly collections, to Stephen Doig and Paul Green for the sketch opposite the foreword by President Mandela, and to Conservation Corporation, Brenthurst Library, JBP Photo Library, ABPL Photo Library, Transnet Heritage Foundation, Museum Africa, National Botanical Gardens, Kirstenbosch and the Transvaal Museum for pictures and their kind assistance.

Molly and I wish to thank the many people who gave up their time to reminisce about their Londolozi days all of whom are named in the roll of honour. We appreciate the assistance given by Nan Trollip, daughter of Frank Unger, Steve Sanders from the U.S. and Ian Whyte of the National Parks.

It is my deep hope that this book will inspire the generations of the future to work together in harmony in keeping the wild areas of Africa and its wonderful biodiversity safe from overdevelopment and exploitation. To the 'bush babies' born at Londolozi and the many children who have visited this wilderness, may your experience influence you to become part of the ever-growing conservation consciousness that is now becoming a worldwide phenomenon.

Shan Varty

W C Harris delt

A LONG TIME AGO

In nature there are neither rewards nor punishments –
there are consequences. — *Robert Green Ingersoll.*

OST GOOD YARNS HAVE A BEGINNING, a middle and an end. This story is different because the end of our story is in fact the beginning. From the first word to the last, all that is recorded in this book is just a preamble to the future – and that story remains untold.

Nature and logic have much in common. Far from progressing in a straight line, they bounce and bump about, sometimes going forwards, sometimes back, as they take apparent anomalies and paradoxes in their stride. They also have a beauty and symmetry, and there appear, at the end, to be no loose ends – although we cannot even begin to understand or fathom the millions of intricacies that have been built into nature's grand design.

The story of Londolozi, so close to nature, follows similar lines. It is a story full of logic and paradoxes: out of hunting came conservation, out of aggression came a passion that would drive a great conservation ethic forward and, in an era torn apart by an ideology of apartheid, great friendships developed between people of different races and cultural backgrounds. To understand these apparent anomalies, it is necessary to go back, not just to 1926 when Charles Varty and Frank Unger bought the farm Sparta in the eastern Transvaal bushveld, but back to the 19th century when this beautiful, untamed land began to give up the struggle for its integrity.

Henry Glynn, in his book *Game and Gold,* wrote about the 1880s, "the country contained game of all descriptions. Black rhinos and white were low down on the Sabi river. Giraffe were all over where the acacia trees were, and buffaloes were found in troops of two to three hundred. I have seen roan antelope, sable, waterbuck and tsessebe and eland in big troops of up to two hundred. Hippos could easily be found in the rivers. Blue wildebeeste and ostrich were plentiful. One day we saw a great many spoors of eland but saw none. We saw, however, seven hunting leopard and the next day we found the eland."

In those early days the twin dragons, the tsetse fly and the mosquito, effectively repulsed persistent efforts to penetrate the bushveld. Alfred Aylward, in his book *The Transvaal of Today* published in 1928 gave an account of the period: "There is in Africa and especially in the Transvaal a closed season when the penalty for descending into the bushveld in search of large game, or of penetrating to the north into the remoter grounds of the elephant hunter is not a fine of five or ten pounds, but the almost certain exposure of the traveller to fever and death."

By the 1860s hunters attracted by the teeming herds of game and the spoils – ivory, hides, meat and trophies – had learnt to make use of the dry winter season. A few decades later the big game, elephants, rhinoceros and buffalo, had almost entirely been driven back into the depths of the 'fly' country;

Above: Bokmakierie (*Telophorus zeylonus*) and redbilled hornbill (*Tockus erythrorhynchus*) from Le Vaillant's *Histoire Naturelle des Oiseaux d'Afrique* published in the last century.
Left: *Leo capensis* - 1883: Engraving from *Brehm's Thierleben* by Dr. A.E. Brehm.

Above: The blue buck which became extinct about 1800 and right, the quagga, last seen 100 years ago. Conservationists estimate that with the disappearance of natural habitat all over the world the destruction of biodiversity will escalate from the present loss of one species a day up to 130 species every 24 hours.

Right below: Kudu much sought after for trophies in earlier times have increased in numbers significantly while rhinoceros, particularly black, would probably already be extinct but for the work of the Natal Parks Board.

Below: Giraffe, whose hides were in much demand during the ox-wagon era have increased in numbers since the advent of the automobile.

giraffe had become scarce although there were still a large number of greater and lesser antelope.

Alfred Aylward went on to say that "as the country has become more settled, a wonderful diminution in the quantity of game in the Transvaal has taken place. This still continues; and if sportsmen want to 'do' Africa they had better make haste, as at the present rate of decrease, in a very few years wild animals, with the exception of springbuck and perhaps blesbuck, will have ceased to exist in this territory. From a sportsman's point of view, great and wanton destruction of game has been going on in some African districts for many years. At one time the veld swarmed with countless herds of antelope of nearly every class and species. Quaggas were to be heard and seen in small troops nearly everywhere; and the land was fairly overrun with 'welderbeests' blue and black, blesbucks, springbucks and many varieties of the less gregarious antelope; but they have been fairly shot off. The farmers stated, I think with reason, that the larger game were subject to diseases which contaminated their herds. They were also shot down in every direction for the sake of their skins, of which I am ashamed to say how many hundred thousand were sent down for sale to the shippers in Natal."

Long before the turn of the century the quagga had been hunted into extinction. Legislation plodded slowly behind and it was not until three years after the last quagga died in the Amsterdam Zoo that laws were passed in 1886 protecting the extinct species. Giraffe, too, nearly disappeared from southern Africa. The long hides were in great demand for 'riems', the strips of raw hide used to inspan oxen at a time when virtually the only mode of transport in southern Africa was the ox-wagon.

The first conservation laws of the Transvaal were not aimed at protecting species but rather at reducing the categories of people permitted to hunt. Thus the indigenous communities, which had for centuries survived as subsistence hunters, were legislated into the role of 'poachers', cutting them off from the economic benefits of their heritage and forcing them into cattle farming which was to do untold ecological damage to the land.

The Transvaal, at that time, was in a political tug-of-war between the Boers under President Kruger and the British. Although the first Europeans to arrive north of the Vaal river (the river that was always dirty-brown with mud) were a few traders and missionaries, the first real settlers of the Transvaal were the Boers who had trekked away from British domination in the Cape. They formed a republic, but this was annexed by Great Britain in April 1877. Five years later after the battle of Majuba where the Boers routed the British redcoats, the South African Republic's independence was restored. But the conflict was not over. Throughout the 1880s small discoveries of gold were made in the Transvaal – at Eersteling north of Pretoria, in the western Transvaal and at

Above: Building of the railway line through the Elands river valley to Komatipoort and Moçambique was completed in 1894. The line made it possible to reach the lowveld without ox-wagon transport which was slow and erratic because the oxen were vulnerable to the deadly disease *Trypanosoma* or sleeping sickness carried by tsetse flies (below).

Right above: The old NZASM railway line to Lourenço Marques.

Right below: A railway bridge near Ladysmith, Natal, which was blown up by the Boers on 25 November 1899. Churchill had been captured very near this bridge 10 days earlier.

Lydenburg and Pilgrim's Rest in the east. These were simply the overture to the fabulous discovery of gold on the Witwatersrand which set in motion events leading to the Boer War. After a conflict of nearly three years, the British again annexed the Transvaal Republic in 1902. Not until 1910, when the Union of South Africa came into being and Louis Botha was called upon to form the first Union ministry, were the Afrikaans leaders back in government.

Only the most determined traveller or prospector was prepared to undergo the hardships and difficulties of travelling by ox-wagon, so graphically described in Percy Fitzpatrick's tale *Jock of the Bushveld*. But, as with the rest of South Africa, the steam train was revolutionising transport. President Kruger, determined to break the British economic stranglehold on his landlocked Republic, planned a route from Pretoria to Delagoa Bay through the Portuguese territory of Moçambique. In 1890 there were 41 miles of rail in the Transvaal. This figure doubled in 1891 and again in 1892. By 1894, when the line to Lourenço Marques, through Komatipoort and the bushveld, was opened, the Transvaal had 573 miles of line. Barry Ronan who worked on the construction said that laying the track had been costly both in money and in men's lives. Lourenço Marques was surrounded by a mosquito-infested belt of swamp forty miles broad and, with nothing known of malarial infection which the mosquito carried, some hundreds of men died during the first year he was there. It was said that a corpse lay under every sleeper of the line.

In 1909, just before Union, the Transvaal decided to spend some of its accumulated wealth rather than have it spread among the other provinces which would be its future partners. One of their projects was to extend the line from Komatipoort northwards over the Sabie river, passing close to the Sand river on its way through the Sabie Game Reserve and to Tzaneen, servicing the goldfields which had opened in the north-eastern Transvaal. This became known as the Selati line and was used by the pioneers travelling to the bushveld.

Winston Churchill gave his view of the subcontinent's transport system: "Railway travelling in South Africa is more expensive but just as comfortable as in India. Lying-down accommodation is provided for all, and meals could be obtained at convenient stopping places." A few years later, in December 1899, he was to travel in much less comfortable circumstances as an escaped prisoner of war. Churchill, at the time a war correspondent for the *Morning Post*, climbed over the wall of the prison camp and walked unchallenged through Pretoria. He then launched himself onto the first goods train that passed by. Before dawn the next day he jumped from the train near a coal mine outside Witbank. By some extraordinary chance he chose to seek help at the only home within 20 miles where he would have received a sympathetic reception. After spending the rest of the week in hiding, he was given a berth on the train bound for Komatipoort and Lourenço Marques.

Top: Komatipoort – the junction of the Lourenço Marques and Selati lines. It was also where travellers changed to ox-wagon transport for journeys south.

Above: Enforcing the anti-poaching laws, several policemen once found themselves totally outclassed. Caught red-handed Judas Mathebula managed to get a message through to his friends to have a plentiful supply of beer at the village where they would spend the night on their way from the Sabie Game Reserve to the magistrate at Bushbuckridge. The policemen imbibed freely and when they were asleep Judas found the keys to his handcuffs, freed himself, then handcuffed the policemen, threw the keys away and destroyed all evidence of his poaching. He then disappeared into the bush. The wily poacher, famous for his hunting skills, was the uncle of Winnis Mathebula who became a great friend of the Varty family and teacher to Dave and John.

President Kruger, Oom Paul to the Boers, played a major role in the events leading up to the second Anglo-Boer War despite his years. He was 75 when he left South Africa in September 1900, taking the train from Pretoria to Lourenço Marques before embarking for Europe. There are two schools of thought as to the role he played in establishing the eastern Transvaal reserves: whether he was pressurised by conservationists or whether it was his decision that finally swayed the Volksraad to proclaim the Sabie Game Reserve. It cannot be denied that Kruger was a strong leader and it would seem more likely that he saw the logic of proclaiming a reserve – and was more likely to sway others than be browbeaten against his will into any decision. If this supposition is correct he deserves all credit for the reserve which bears his name.

Not long after that President Kruger, possibly with some of the fabled 'Kruger millions', made his escape from the British, travelling the same route through the Sabie Game Reserve, which two decades later was to bear his name. The gold bars and coins, which legend claims were taken from Pretoria to a place of safety before the end of the Boer War, have excited much speculation over the past century. One rumour suggests that the bullion was taken from Komatipoort up the Selati line to Skukuza and buried in the present day Sabi Sand reserve. Another, that it was loaded into a ship in Delagoa Bay but, soon after sailing, the ship was wrecked on the Zululand coast. To this day the whereabouts of the Boer Republic's treasure, or if it even exists, remains a mystery.

In 1896 the rinderpest struck. This virulent disease attacked the respiratory systems of cattle, buffalo, wildebeest and other ungulates and was one of the greatest disasters ever to befall South Africa. It swept through the country from end to end, destroying cattle and all but exterminating the wildebeest population of the eastern Transvaal. To add to the disaster, the destruction of wildlife, which was considered a carrier of the virus, was actively encouraged. Had it not been for the railway line through Komatipoort, transport through the bushveld, which had previously only been possible by ox-wagon, would have been paralysed. But some good came out of the disaster. In the aftermath of rinderpest it was discovered that, along with the massive loss of cattle and game, the tsetse fly had disappeared and with it the dreaded sleeping sickness.

President Kruger, a fine shot and fearless hunter, first announced his concern about the wholesale slaughter of wildlife for commercial gain in 1884, the year after he became President of the Transvaal Republic. He said: "It is becoming advisable to set aside some kind of sanctuary in which game may find a refuge." At that time the Transvaal Republic was on the verge of bankruptcy. Two years later the Boers' world was turned up-side-down by the discovery of the Witwatersrand goldfield. 'Uitlanders' (foreigners) flocked into the Republic bringing one problem after another to the President. Many people with powerful agricultural interests would have preferred to use the lowveld for cattle ranching. However, despite the many crises, in 1898, a year before the outbreak of the Anglo Boer War, the Volksraad (People's Council) under President Kruger, proclaimed a game reserve "daar onder by die Sabierivier" (down by the Sabie river), where no hunting or shooting would be allowed.

After the end of the Boer War in 1902, Lieutenant Colonel James Stevenson-Hamilton was appointed to care for the Sabie Game Reserve. A man way ahead of his time, he was a Scot born in Ireland and educated in England. He was first a hunter and then a naturalist with a keen understanding and concern for what he termed the balance of nature.

His early years in the Sabie Game Reserve were by no means smooth going. It was a case of shutting the stable door after the horse had bolted. So many animals had been lost over the previous 40 years that rebuilding the wildlife populations was a major priority. Stevenson-Hamilton's first concern was to ensure that the game reserve was firmly established on the country's statute books. Under his direction the original reserve which fell between the Sabie and Crocodile rivers was extended north up to the Olifants river and linked to the Shingwedzi Game Reserve between the Letaba and Pafuri rivers, laying the foundation for the two-million-hectare Kruger National Park. The initial proclamation in 1903 over the enlarged area covered a period of only five years. This was extended several times. In January 1913 just before its expiry the reserve's administration asked for two more years in which to formulate a definite policy but another 11 years was to pass before the Park was eventually proclaimed.

Many conflicting interests were involved, primarily because about one-fifth of the seven-million-acre Sabie Game Reserve was privately owned. Transvaal Consolidated Land & Exploration Company (TCL), the largest of the private landowners, rated their 516 000 acres within the Sabie Game Reserve as "very valuable and highly suitable for cattle ranching, cotton growing and all subtropical crops, including fruit". Development plans were first postponed by World War I. After the war, as was reported in the TCL annual accounts in the 1920s, it was discovered that their valuable asset could not be used: "There were no fences to keep out elephants and larger antelope and during the 18 years prior to 1922 the number of lions had grown from two to three hundred to something over three thousand. Similarly the proportion of hunting dogs, jackals and leopards had grown, and this vermin is a menace to stock owners."

During 1921 efforts were made by private landowners to abolish the Sabie Game Reserve and when these failed, TCL decided to put the government's game protection programme to the test. In 1923 the company moved some 800 head of cattle onto the farm Toulon within the Sabie Game Reserve. Mr. A.J. Crosby, the manager, was instructed to assert the company's rights of ownership and, after discussion with Stevenson-Hamilton with whom he was on friendly terms, he went out and shot a lone wildebeest bull on the grounds "that it was eating the company grass reserved for the cattle". A summons was issued but at the end of the court case, the magistrate found against the company.

To meet the farmers' demands half way, and probably more significantly, to limit the cost of land settlements, in 1923 the Sabie Game Reserve's western border was redrawn to the east, reducing the reserve's area by just over a million acres. Many private farms then fell outside the reserve's border including some 312 000 acres owned by TCL. As a result, the farms Sparta, Toulon, Charleston, Flockfield, Mala Mala and Marthly along the Sand river, the heart of the present day Sabi Sand Wildtuin, fell outside the park.

Those farms not immediately bordering the Kruger National Park were described ominously in the title deeds as within a 'Released Area'. This meant

Colonel James Stevenson-Hamilton believed that one of the objectives of a reserve was to allow wildlife to follow their habits without interference by man. On his retirement in 1946, gradually a new philosophy took over – management by intervention. Some 50 years later the *laissez-faire* approach of non-intervention gathers momentum. Below, wildebeest.

that the National Party under General J.B. Hertzog, which had come into power in 1924, could, at a later date, claim the land for African resettlement. It was stated at the time that provided certain conditions were complied with, this clause in the agreement would be excised. Many years later in 1973, when the apartheid policy of homeland resettlement got underway, this clause was to give owners of Sabi Sand farms some anxiety – despite the fact that the conditions had been met.

The same year, Sir William Hoy, general manager of South African Railways, decided to use the eastern Transvaal and the Sabie Game Reserve to promote rail travel. A round trip of nine days taking in Nelspruit, Sabie, Graskop, Tzaneen and then through the reserve to Komatipoort was advertised. About 100 people visited the park that year. This figure had grown to some 850 000 by 1995. Stevenson-Hamilton, according to Madeleine Varty, "would have preferred to have kept the reserve for wildlife", but the visitors did much to increase the public's awareness of the beauty of the reserve and to head off its plight as another opportunity for 'farms and factories'.

The way was now open for Mr. P.G.W. Grobler, Minister of Lands and a relative of Paul Kruger, to pilot the National Parks Bill through parliament. This he achieved in 1926 when he proposed a non-political National Parks Board to regulate and control the Kruger National Park. On the board was William Alfred Campbell, Wac to his friends, who the following year bought the farm Mala Mala which became one of South Africa's great hunting estates during his lifetime.

By 1926 TCL had matters other than farming on its agenda. The German-born geologist Hans Merensky, had discovered platinum in the Lydenburg district and this had stimulated the company to spend large amounts on prospecting, not only for platinum but also for tin, asbestos and mica, while its ranching activities were making heavy losses. The decision was taken to sell off much of their farmland which, after the proclamation of the Kruger National Park, fell outside the reserve. This set off a chain of events that led almost half a century later to the development of Londolozi Game Reserve.

By 1934 all TCL farms in the area had been sold, although ranching continued on Toulon until 1938 when foot-and-mouth disease necessitated shooting the entire herd. On the Sabi Sand boundary cattle rotational grazing schemes under the homeland system are still very much with us, even though in these low rainfall areas they are an ecological disaster and, historically, cattle ranching has been proved to be both unsustainable and unprofitable.

In 1927 Harry Kirkman took over from Crosby as TCL's farm manager, remaining there until he moved to the Kruger National Park in 1933. During these years his major task had been to look after company cattle. Harry believed that he could kill two birds with one stone: he could protect his cattle and at the same time conserve wildlife if he controlled the carnivore. Even into the 1980s

Above, a lioness at the Sand river, and opposite, a kudu cow at sunset.

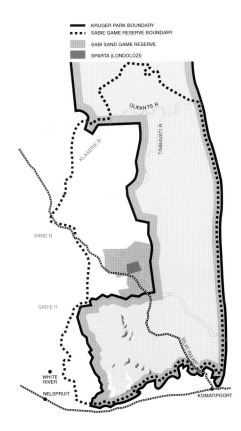

The western boundary of the Sabie Game Reserve was shifted to the east in 1923. As a result the farm Sparta fell outside the reserve area which three years later was to become the Kruger National Park.

when he was getting on in years, he would say: "You've got too many lions – they're eating all your game. Shoot the lions!" He was reputed to have shot over 1200 lions. He shot them in the day, he shot them in the night, he shot them on horseback and on foot. Then in the mid-60s while tracking a wounded lion on behalf of one of the owners of Sabi Sand, he was severely mauled. He managed to get back to his house from where he phoned the doctor in Skukuza, asking: "Have you got anything for lion bite?" Harry was tough. He recovered.

Harry Kirkman was one of the great characters amongst those pioneering men. He was scrupulously honest, straight as a die, unable to put on airs or graces, and was both an extraordinary observer of nature and of character. He was not alone in his belief that lions were better dead than alive. The Transvaal Game Protection Association, formed in 1902, had a membership of about 1000 by 1906. The objectives of the association were primarily: "to promote the interests of sportsmen in South Africa, to bring about destruction of vermin (which is how they described carnivore), to extend their knowledge of wildlife and to see that existing laws for the protection of game were enforced and observed". In those days sportsmen neither compared hunting, regulated by a strict code of ethics, with the wholesale slaughter of game for commercial exploitation nor did they have any scientific knowledge of the close link between species and ecology. In fact the National Parks Board did not have a scientific member until the 1940s.

An account of the Transvaal Game Protection Association's activities gives some idea of the thinking at the time. In league with the Department of Agriculture, the Association offered rewards for the destruction of carnivore and poisonous snakes.

Back in Johannesburg in 1926, two friends, Charles Varty and Frank Unger, were made aware of the changes taking place in the eastern Transvaal. Over a game of tennis they discussed the opportunity of buying their own hunting preserve. One of their tennis-playing friends, Major Percy Greathead, was estates manager for TCL. He knew the Sand river area well and probably would have told the two men more about the farm Sparta which his company had decided to sell. It was close to the newly established Kruger National Park and TCL's cattle ranch, Toulon. Of particular significance was that the sale also included a section of the farm, Marthly which linked Sparta to the Sand river.

Frank and Charles had much in common. Besides enjoying cricket and tennis, they were both engineers, and had a great love of nature and spirit of adventure. Frank was a mining engineer and ended up as deputy chairman of Anglo American. Charles Varty had grown up in the Natal midlands. His grandfather Arthur had left England in the 1850s and settled at Rietvlei in the Karkloof near the majestic Drakensberg range. He and his two brothers had raised cattle and then introduced sheep to the area which was a disaster. They

Harry Kirkman arrived in the bushveld in 1926 and became one of the great pioneering characters of the time. An uncanny marksman, lion hunter and superb horseman, he dedicated his life to the care of the wilderness. He was a role model for John and Dave Varty.

Right: Rewards were offered by the so-called Transvaal Game Protection Association: £10 for the destruction of lions (skull above), £5 for leopards, £2 10s for hyenas and hunting dogs, 2s 6d each for mambas, cobras and berg adders and 1s each for all other poisonous snakes.

then tried diamond digging but the first two attempts in the eastern Transvaal ended in abysmal failure. Then they joined the rush to Colesberg, near Kimberley, where they were successful.

Charles was only 14 when his father died at the early age of 38. His uncle William helped him finish his schooling and he joined Stewarts & Lloyds, an engineering concern with its head office in Scotland. From an office boy in Pietermaritzburg he ultimately became managing director of the company's South African operations. Madeleine Varty, Charles's daughter-in-law, says of him: "He took his responsibilities very seriously caring for his mother and his sisters from an early age. He was never what one would call a wealthy man, and when he bought his share of Sparta he paid it off bit by bit."

By then the mosquito had been identified as the carrier of malaria and only the foolhardy travelled to the bushveld during the summer months. So, rather than miss the opportunity to purchase what their friends considered was a disease-ridden, back-of-beyond piece of real estate, Charles and Frank went ahead and bought the 10 000 acre farm sight unseen for the grand sum of £1236.11.5d, equivalent today to just under 25 cents an acre. That winter they set off on their expedition of discovery.

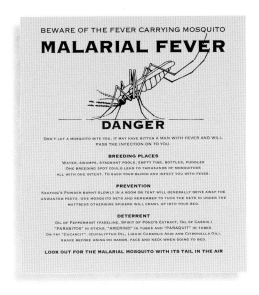

Left: The farm Sparta perceived as a disease-ridden, back-of-beyond piece of African real estate.

THE PIONEERING YEARS

Man and antelope. Man and lion. Hunter and hunted.
Our future and our past are inseparable. — *Creina Bond.*

HE JOURNEY TO SPARTA 70 years ago would be quite a shattering experience for today's visitors who travel to Londolozi in absolute comfort and convenience. Charles and Frank's expedition in July 1926 started relatively easily, but did not end so. There were no beacons or landmarks to show them the way, no accommodation waiting for them, no comfortable bed, no shower and no hot water. They had only what they took with them; a tent to protect them from the elements and their guns – and when they got there, an icy river to swim in, carefully watching out for crocodile and hippo.

The steam train from the Witwatersrand passed through Waterval Boven and down a perilous pass into the beautiful Elands river valley; then on to Nelspruit and Komatipoort where they would have spent a cold winter's night before taking the Selati line north through the wild and uninhabited reserve. The line passed close to the Sand river, through Toulon and the south-west corner of Sparta on its way to Tzaneen. Bert Tomlinson, the Toulon ranch manager, had arranged for a party of bearers to await the two men between milestones 61 and 62 where they would leave the train and start walking in a north-easterly direction towards the Sand river about five miles away.

Imagine the excitement – the sheer exhilaration of being there first! When they stopped to catch their breath, they would have heard the birds and the insects which at sunrise and sunset create such an unforgettable cacophony of sound. They would have caught glimpses of roan and sable antelope, eland, waterbuck and wildebeest, and perhaps heard the distant – and often not so distant – earth-moving roar of lion. For both it was the start of a love affair that would last a lifetime.

Initially there was no time for relaxation. They had a long way to go and a heavy load to carry. Madeleine Varty recounts the tale: "The rendezvous was kept and after the bearers had taken up their loads, the two white nkosi led them into the bush. They were armed with two rifles, a compass and a rough sketch map of the area. Three-quarters of the way there the bearers mutinied and threw down their loads. Where was the water the nkosi had promised? They were being led further and further into the bush to die of thirst."

Charles, having grown up in Natal, had learnt to speak Zulu as a child and was able to converse easily with the Shangaan bearers. When he arrived home he told his children: "If the men had left us then, we would have been forced to give up. Just to get out would have been a herculean task. But after much bargaining, coaxing and convincing, one of the bearers named Five set himself up as cheerleader. With stories, songs, jokes and antics, he persuaded his team to continue and trust the nkosi with their piece of paper and queer-looking charm (the compass) that showed them the way." From later stories told by

Top: A blackbellied korhaan *Eupodotis melanogaster*, also called a langbeen-(long-legged) korhaan and centre, one of thousands of 'bug' species: a leafhopper of the family Cicadellidae. Above, an army surplus compass from World War I.

Opposite: A group of waterbuck cows in the tall grass in summer.

Above: Impala and kudu.

Opposite: Rhino had been plentiful in the lowveld in the last century but had disappeared from the Sand river area along with elephant. In 1965 Loring Rattray, owner of the farm Exeter on the Sand river upstream from Sparta, imported two pairs of white rhino from the Umfolozi Reserve and a year later the first calf was born. As a result of these and other imports, today these magnificent prehistoric animals are well established throughout the area.

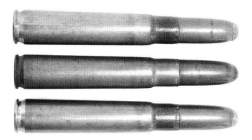

Harry Kirkman, it is quite likely that Five was simply putting the nkosi to the test. Less than an hour later they reached the banks of the Sand river where the water runs clear over granite rocks and where Sparta camp – and now Londolozi – stands to this day.

It was unique. It was beautiful. Peaceful. Remote. And, best of all, it was theirs. Before the sun set there was still work to be done; setting up camp, fetching water from the river, collecting firewood and making a fire to last the night so as to keep away predators. Not least there was dinner to cook. After their first meal, sitting under that wonderful, starry bushveld sky, in the glow of the fire, they must have felt a joy and a sense of peace that comes to those who lose themselves to the beauty of the African wilderness.

In the South African bushveld there is no massive migration of animals from south to north as in the Masai Mara grasslands of Kenya and the Serengeti of Tanzania. Between the Olifants and Sabie rivers, the wildebeest and zebra move leisurely, generally north-west into the short grass plains of the Timbavati area following summer's erratic rainfall pattern in an endless search for food. Then as winter sets in and their summer grazing has been exhausted, they move back south-east until they reach the grasslands of what is now the Sabi Sand reserve and the permanent water supply of the Sand and Sabie rivers. There was also a well-established population of sedentary species; waterbuck, reedbuck, sable and tsessebe and the smaller antelope such as duiker and steenbok. In those days no fences restricted this natural movement of game towards water and grazing. Frank and Charles had arrived in July when the migratory species had already concentrated in their winter habitat along the Sand river. Hard on their heels followed a large contingent of predators.

Winter in the bushveld is a wonderful season. The dry, golden grass, full of nutrients for the animals, is soon grazed short, so that, in the days before bush encroachment, it would have been possible to see large herds of sable, sometimes nearly 200, with relative ease. The days are sunny and warm, but soon after the sun sets, one is reminded that it is winter. Some years it would be really freezing, and on one occasion in 1953, Skukuza recorded more than ten degrees of frost.

Both Charles and Frank were excellent shots. They would have set out before dawn on their first hunt on Sparta. The area was teeming with game, wonderfully exciting and totally fascinating. In her history of the Sabi Sand Madeleine Varty wrote: "That first camp of Charles and Frank was conducted in a manner that has been followed ever since: an early morning hunt, camp chores, lunch and perhaps a siesta until the sun lost its sting. After 4 o'clock another hunt or walk through the bushveld untouched and untrammelled by the feet of man since the beginning of time. Then a campfire, gun-cleaning and a drink and – in later years – a swapping of hunters' yarns."

Five Nyalunga, the original guide lent to Charles and Frank, was TCL's top Shangaan tracker. Typical of the people of Africa, he had spent his entire life as a hunter/gatherer, living in harmony with wildlife as his forefathers had done for many generations. At the turn of the century his traditional occupation had been outlawed and he had taken a job at Toulon, protecting the company's 2500 head of cattle from the persistent attacks by lions. He would have taught Frank and Charles all he knew about the wildlife of the region: how to follow a spoor and to interpret the tracks, to listen to the birds, not just their songs, but their signals of concern and alarm which were of much more interest to hunters. During their first visit they met a ranger from the Kruger National Park who suggested they permanently employ one of his trackers, Winnis Mathebula, who was to become a friend and instructor to three generations of the Varty family.

Before dawn broke, over a mug of hot coffee, Frank and Charles would have heard the sharp alarm call of impala, the eerie call of hyena or the roar of lions; and then in the soft light before dawn they would have followed the spoor.

"Lion hunting was part of a long tradition not only in our own family but throughout Africa's early history," comments Dave Varty, grandson of Charles and co-founder with his brother John of Londolozi. "It called for total involvement of all the senses – of sight, sound and smell – and for an enormous fund of energy and courage. The hunting ethics practised by my grandfather were instilled in us as children: how to handle a gun, to go out at first light and only on foot, with no vehicles and no telescopic sights. We never shot a female, only males and if we wounded an animal we went after it at all costs. We never used lights or bait. We were taught to listen to the sounds of the wild, gleaning information from the bush telegraph system and were always alert and totally committed. To get up close to a lion we had to be very, very quiet. This was not so easy for me. I have memories of getting many a clip on the ear because I was so clumsy and could never stop coughing. Dad used to say I sounded like a baby elephant." A stifled cough was not funny when hunting lions. It could quite easily be mistaken for the low grunt of a lion and as Dave recalls: "You could suddenly find three or four guns trained on you.

"Following a spoor on foot was always high drama and exciting; many dangerous situations could develop and some were hair-raising. We learnt to listen holding our breath," Dave said. "Impala alarm calls, chattering squirrels, a particular call from a grey lourie – there would be a lot of information coming to us. Night traffic on top of the spoor of animals we were tracking and dew in the pad marks would give us an indication of time, the sharpness of the spoor and if it was scuffed would give us an idea of how fast the animal was moving, while alarm calls ahead would tell us how far away we were from the pride.

"Winnis had what could be termed second sight when it came to animals. His observations and understanding of game were uncanny. He would stop and

Dave Varty remembers his father, Boyd, (above and left) telling him of the occasion when Winnis Mathebula, one of the great naturalists and hunters of his day, came and sat at his feet in a really tight spot. Winnis wasn't going anywhere. Between them they had seven shots, two in Winnis's shotgun and five in Boyd's rifle. But 20 lions were around them, all threatening, lashing their tails and looking decidedly hungry! Winnis became trusted friend and teacher to three generations of the Varty family.

Above: The grey lourie, *Corythaixoides concolor,* commonly known as the 'go-away' bird because of its loud 'go-way' screech, and impala with their sharp alarm calls, would give an early warning to hunters if predators were about.

Opposite: Lion prowling around the cattle kraal would be undeterred by warning shots fired over their heads.

listen for an alarm call. Listen for a second call – perhaps of a kudu calling from another direction – and take us at a hell of a pace to a spot that would intersect the route taken by lion. There we would sit down and wait, listening to the alarm calls coming closer and closer and with the tension mounting every second. Sometimes the lions would disappear into a thick riverine patch. We would then have several options, first of all to circle the bush. If there were no tracks leaving the area we would go back for breakfast. Then in the heat of the day, when the cats were asleep we would crawl into the thick bush until we could catch a glimpse of a lion's tawny coat. If we could see one we knew others would be lying around and very close. Then we would manoeuvre for a shot. We would not go for a female or cubs. Hopefully a male would sit up or jump up and we would have a split second to take a shot. In that thick bush all hell would break loose. If we hit a lion, it could come at us or it might run. And everywhere lions would jump up, snarling, growling and threatening – from only a few metres away. In those few seconds the adrenaline flowed – it was unbelievable. That's what lion hunting was all about.

"There was a distinct difference between hunting in those days and nowadays, when for the most part it has become an exercise in the collection of big trophies," said Dave. "We never looked for records, it was man against animal, part of our ancient heritage. And if you kept your wits you would survive."

The following year, in July 1927, Frank and Charles were determined that their families would share their experience. Once again they took the train to Komatipoort, sleeping overnight before travelling on the Selati line, this time to the siding at Toulon where they spent a second night. The following morning Harry Kirkman, who had been appointed farm manager at Toulon earlier that year, inspanned an ox-wagon lent by TCL, and together with five or six milk-cows they set off through the bush for their camp at Sparta. The cows were an important part of the cavalcade as they were to provide milk and butter for the children. In later years they found it easier to take goats, but the lions found the goats easy picking too!

There were many nights when Frank and Charles would have to protect their cows, terrified by the smell and sound of lions prowling just outside their kraal. They would shoot over the heads of the lions to chase them away. Sometimes they were in time, sometimes they were not. John Varty remembers one incident of those early years: "My grandfather was travelling to Sparta via Machado-dorp and Bushbuckridge where he had hired an ox-wagon for the month. Just after sunset they heard a terrific commotion towards the front of the span. My father, Boyd, just 14 years old at the time, used to repeat the story to us every time we came to the crossing of the river. He had held up the kerosene lamp to reveal a lion attacking the lead ox. Charles hastily grabbed his rifle and was able to dispatch the lion, but not before it had killed the unfortunate ox."

The upper and undersides of *Precis tugela*,
the African leaf commodore and upper side
of *Precis archesia*, the garden commodore
or garden inspector.

Above: A lion yawns and displays his fear-some weapons: the deadly canines for throttling and killing, the incisors for stripping meat and the carnassails and molars adapted to cutting rather than crushing.

Opposite: Above, Frank Unger (right) with his brother Jan (left), Winnis Mathebula, a friend and a tracker, about 1933. Below left: The station at Komatipoort where the Varty and Unger families spent the night before taking the train on the Selati line to Skukuza and to within 15 miles of Sparta. Below right: When the Unger and Varty families first visited Sparta their only accommodation was tents which were set up within a thorn-bush boma to give some protection from the lions.

Feathers of the woodland kingfisher.

That first party consisted of Frank Unger, his wife Clarice and their three eldest daughters, Betty, Claire and Phyllis, and Charles Varty, his wife, Mizpah, their son, Boyd and his sisters, Helen and Nan.

The previous season Charles and Frank had built a thornbush boma to give the party some protection from wild animals, but apart from the long-drop built several hundred metres away, facilities were non-existent. Nan Trollip, the youngest of the Unger sisters, first visited Sparta a few years later when she was three. "My mother, sister Claire, our English nanny and I took the train to Komatipoort where we spent the night before travelling on the Selati line to Toulon. The men had gone ahead to set up camp and my mother was terrified that there would be no one to meet us at the Toulon siding. There was absolutely nothing there, not one building. Fortunately her fears were groundless. The men were waiting for us and we set off in an ox-wagon for Sparta and for what would be our home for a month.

"I don't know how my mother and Mrs. Mizpah Varty managed. By the time I went down there in 1929 we had located a supplier in White River who helped set up camp for us. As well as tents, he would deliver our vegetables for a month – all root vegetables, potatoes, onions, turnips, carrots – which were put into a hole in the ground to keep fresh. Our fridge was a cupboard with chicken-wire front and sides over which a wet cloth or piece of sacking was draped. The breeze kept the food reasonably cool. At least we did have fresh milk and butter and bread was baked every day.

"Our mothers kept frightfully high standards, everything correctly served and they were always properly dressed – well, almost always. I remember on one occasion we were bathing in a pool down by the river, a secluded spot, protected by tall reeds. Suddenly our ablutions were interrupted by the roar of a lion, very, very close. My mother charged out from her private pool clad only in a long pair of striped bloomers, swept us all up and raced us past the guard and back to camp. Towels and toothbrushes went down the river. Can you imagine how embarrassing it must have been for a woman brought up in full Victorian tradition! We girls found it embarrassing being escorted to the long-drop, but it was very necessary to have a guard. Over the years everything from a lion to a mamba was found inside the enclosure."

Nan Trollip says of her father: "Coming from Holland, an overcrowded Europe and bad weather, my father was seduced by Africa. I don't think there was anybody I knew who so appreciated that pristine bushveld and the wonderful sunshine. He really did instil into us just how precious Sparta was. He recognised that there would be great pressure on that wonderful land and urged us to preserve our heritage at all cost. He loved the animals, loved walking and observing everything that crawled or flew, and although he was a good shot, he only killed for the pot."

The beautiful fruitchafer or cetoniine, *Dichronorhina derbyana*, is attracted to sapping trees and fermenting fruit; and *Anthia thoracica*, one of the largest groundbeetles of southern Africa, is predacious on many other ground insects.

Locusts, which caused one of the plagues of Egypt, fly strongly and travel considerable distances until they find suitable vegetation which they voraciously destroy.

Harry Wolhuter, in his book *Memories of a Game Ranger,* recounts that the area along the western boundary, which in 1926 fell outside the Kruger National Park's sphere of control, became a prime target for poachers. He estimated that about 3000 head of game were killed during the first three years after the boundary line was redrawn – "including the less common types such as roan and sable antelope and reedbuck". Harry Kirkman, while waging a war against lion to protect his cattle, was an ardent lover of the wilderness and of wildlife. He believed there was grass enough for his cattle and all the game. In 1928 he appointed two Shangaan game rangers, Shoes and Masodja, who, armed with their long assegais, took on the formidable task of combating game poaching. Shoes and Masodja, wonderful hunters in their own right, thus became the first conservation officers of the Sabi Sand.

Dave Varty recalls: "Many of our staff had wonderful names. There was Lice, one of twins who were probably named 'Prunes and Rice'. Masodja was tall and dark. His name was the Shangaan word for the long, black mopane worm. There was Spook and Knife, two of our cooks, and some great trackers, Nkentshane (meaning wild dog), Snotice, Tie, Shoes, Sandwich, Fixo, Pencil, Judas, Engine and Two-tone whose father had intended to call his son Two-stroke. And there was the indestructible and fearless Winnis Mathebula, one of the great hunters and trackers of his day. Winnis worked for our family for 50 years. The camaraderie and trust that developed between tracker and hunter was a bond that remained for life. Winnis was first a friend to our grandfather and to our father. Then when John and I were growing up in the bushveld he became everything to us, philosopher and storyteller, teacher, great naturalist and friend.

"Winnis took great enjoyment in recounting the tale of when Tie tried to shoot a charging lioness at 20 yards – and left the safety catch on. Stephen Roche had shot the lioness clean through the heart at 120 yards, but she kept on coming straight through them and only dropped dead 50 yards beyond. Each time we came to a certain spot in the bush where it happened, Winnis would re-enact the whole drama: 'Kudala skat,' (A long time ago) he would start and we would know we were in for several hours of story telling during which time he would make sure that we appreciated that he, Winnis Mathebula, would never have been such an idiot!"

The 1928/29 summer was the last wet season for many years. Once again, as so often happens in Africa, disasters do not arrive singly but in their droves. The next five years brought drought, high temperatures fanned by hot winds that shrivelled everything under the sun, and to add to their misery the Great Depression and its companions of poverty and unemployment. And then, if this were not enough, locusts arrived; great clouds of insects that devoured every bit of greenery wherever and whenever they settled.

It was small wonder that Transvaal Consolidated Lands had had enough of ranching. Despite Harry's war on lions, cattle were continually being lost while disease took its toll of cattle in poor condition because of the drought. By 1934 TCL had sold off most of its farms to private owners and Harry Kirkman had moved across to the Kruger National Park. In 1938 foot-and-mouth disease appeared in the lowveld, and if TCL had not closed their ranching operations earlier, this would have finished things off. It was the end of the era of cattle ranching within the wedge of land between the Sabie and Sand rivers, an era which had lasted for over 30 years. The veterinary method of combating the disease was simply to shoot all the cattle. Imagine the spectacle of over a thousand head of cattle shot in one day. The graves of these cattle can still be seen alongside the old rail line on Toulon.

Charles and Frank, the first to arrive in the area purely for the enjoyment of the wilderness and the game, were soon followed by others. In 1927 TCL sold Eyrefield to Wac Campbell who later bought Mala Mala and portions of Marthly. The Wilkens family bought the farm Dudley and by 1933 there was quite a community, all of whom visited their farms only in the winter months. According to Madeleine Varty: "They looked for a scheme of co-operative game protection, preferably with a ranger to look after the participating farms. The Transvaal Land Owners' Association, which had been set up to administer unoccupied agricultural and game farms for individuals and groups, was consulted and readily accepted the task. As a result the Sabi Private Game Scheme was formed and Donald Kirkman, a cousin of Harry's, was appointed the first official ranger."

In the early 1930s the motor car was starting to revolutionise transport even in this remote backwater of civilisation. In the early days one had the choice of walking, trekking by ox-wagon or riding on Harry's buckboard drawn by four mules, two of which were tame and two wild. Despite the latter's speed, many people infinitely preferred walking. Nan Varty, young as she was, recalls the 15-mile hurtle through the bush from Toulon to Sparta on the buckboard as one of the most hair-raising experiences of her life. Harry's buckboard virtually took off whenever they hit a bump, and with only a narrow wooden seat, it was rather hard on the fundament!

It was not long before the families were travelling by road from Johannesburg to Skukuza. After 1930, if conditions were right, they were able to cross the rivers and drive on to the Sparta camp. The alternative was taking an ox-wagon from Bushbuckridge. Roads were virtually non-existent. If it was at all wet, the cars would sink into the soft black turf and it would be a long tough job digging them out.

Nan Trollip remembers the awe with which, at the age of three, she first looked up at a giraffe. She recalls the walks through the bush on Sparta: "All the

Above: Betty Unger first visited Sparta in 1927 with two of her sisters and her parents, Frank and Clarice. Sixty years later her son Allan Taylor would inherit half of Sparta and become a partner and great friend to Dave and John Varty.

Below: Madeleine Varty recalls that when Henry Ford II visited the Sabi Sand in the 60s he was not at all impressed with the roads. They had hardly changed since the automobile first made its appearance.

Princess Alice, beautiful and elegant, was also a fine shot. Maidie Varty interviewed the Princess in 1972 when she was on a private visit to Johannesburg almost 50 years after her safari to the bushveld. She remembered the lion hunt with Harry Kirkman and Alex Logan which ended on Sparta "as though it were yesterday".

Opposite: Above, zebra at the Sand river. Below left, the name 'Sparta' imaginatively drawn in an old photo album. Below right, the original thatched rondavels on Sparta.

girls were conservationists, loved the animals and hated hunting." And then in the 1930s wonderful times were had with a camera. "The Americans did this country an enormous favour because they really started the vogue of shooting with a camera," recalls Nan. "To get a really good picture in those days, without telephoto lenses and Land Rovers was quite an achievement. We had such fun, waiting at a waterhole, very patiently and quietly. We had to make sure the wind was right and the animals could neither see, hear nor smell us."

One Sparta camp incident concerned Sally, a golden labrador, who was not a favourite of Madeleine Varty's mother-in-law: "Coming down to the camp fire just after dusk, Mrs. Varty senior inquired of her husband, 'Why didn't you tie up Sally as I asked you?' 'I did tie her up, perhaps she has broken loose. I'll go and see,' Charles volunteered. He discovered the dog still tied up, but in the sand, the unmistakable pug marks of a lion which had made off smartly when the camp's matriarch had flapped a good bright towel at his head!"

Through the 1930s life went on very peacefully in the lowveld. There were few changes. Four thatched mud rondavels made their appearance on Sparta and permanent accommodation was built for the staff. Then as storm clouds gathered in Europe, Charles Varty, always a pioneer, became the first owner to reach his farm by private aircraft. Madeleine Varty recalls the excitement and wonder of the local people when Mr. Varty appeared out of the sky and landed on an airstrip that had been cleared near the railway line on Sparta.

In March 1942 Boyd and Madeleine married. "It was a great sadness for Boyd that we could not spend our honeymoon on his beloved Sparta. We could not go in summer because of malaria," remembers Madeleine. A few months later Boyd and Madeleine managed to spend a week at Sparta and Madeleine began a game book, logging events during their Sparta holidays. She refers to Mgetches (named after a famous bow-and-arrow hunter who had lived in the area), Mshabene and Princess Alice Bush. These were three heavily wooded areas on Sparta favoured by lions because of the dense cover they provided. Princess Alice, a granddaughter of Queen Victoria, visited the eastern Transvaal bushveld in 1932 as a guest of their neighbour, Wac Campbell. She shot and wounded a lion and Harry Kirkman went after it, tracking the lion across the boundary onto Sparta. He finally dispatched the wounded animal in the thick bush which now bears her name. "Her husband," Madeleine recalls, "was a terrible shot and was called a 'bloody fool' by one of the trackers when he totally missed a kudu. Princess Alice was much amused. The Earl of Athlone, Governor General of South Africa at the time, had never been blasphemed to his face before, and probably never would be again."

Madeleine's first entry in her journal reads: "Owing to late rains the grass was unduly long. There were many wild pear trees in blossom. The aloes and palms previously planted at the camps are progressing, and further creepers and

shrubs are to be planted. There were indications of a big pride of 15 to 20 lions at Mgetches but none were actually seen. A lone male was sighted on the Mshabene and we found indications of a pride of three. A leopard was sighted in the riverbed close to Winnis's old home while six lions were spotted across the Sand river."

The following year she wrote: "Seven lions (five lions and two lionesses) and four cubs were run into at Mgetches at a range of thirty yards. The cubs ran between the hunters' legs while the lionesses looked on threateningly. On Monday morning Boyd and Winnis followed a lioness with cubs for some miles on the flats between Mshabene and Mgetches. Eventually she headed for the Mgetches waterhole and because the wind was wrong, the spoor was left. On approaching the reedbed from the southern side, two leopards were heard grumbling at about 15 yards distance."

Those were idyllic times in this pristine wilderness. There were no airplanes overhead. On the ground were only a few almost impassable tracks, and man, the great despoiler, had not yet arrived in large numbers in this north-east corner of South Africa.

Opposite: A leopard keeps watch for larger predators as it takes a drink at the Sand river.

WILD DAYS

There is no wealth but life. — *John Ruskin.*

HERE WERE MANY CHANGES in the lowveld after the war, although life at Sparta went on very much as before with many happy, but some sad, exceptions. Charles Varty contracted pneumonia while on a trip into the Lesotho mountains and died in 1946. Boyd inherited his half-share in Sparta. Two years later Frank Unger died and a new generation, which had known the bushveld almost all their lives, took up their responsibilities as custodians of Sparta. The Unger girls, Betty, Phyllis and Nan suggested that if the farm Charleston, which Frank Unger had also bought, and Sparta were both divided, each of the four beneficiaries could have their own camp. Very soon thereafter Boyd and the Unger girls were each the registered owners of about 2000 hectares of wilderness bordering on the Sand river.

In 1948, an informal gathering of owners of farms in the area between the Sabie and Sand rivers, agreed to change the name of their association to Sabi Sand Wildtuin. A literal translation of Wildtuin is 'wild garden', although it could more appropriately be called a nature reserve. However, the final move to registration as a private nature reserve was only made in 1962.

During the war medical research discovered the means to combat malaria. If not totally able to prevent the disease, the new drugs were at least able to reduce the risk. To this day, the best form of prevention of malaria is to avoid being bitten by mosquitoes. However, the appearance of malarial prophylactics meant that visits to the bushveld were no longer restricted to the winter months.

In July 1948 Claudia Varty made her first appearance at Sparta at ten weeks old, two years later in 1950 Jonathan Varty paid his first visit at seven months, and in May 1954 David Varty visited Sparta when he was just three months old. Helen Varty had married Arthur Thomas and had produced four sons, Grant, Peter, Neil, and Ian, while Nan Varty married Donald Lennard and had three children, Pauline, Stephen and Mark. Wonderful times were had on Sparta. Together the families and their friends visited their wildlife paradise whenever they could and as the children grew up the wild days began.

Madeleine's account of the wildlife recorded in the Sparta Game Book in July 1951 clearly illustrates the massive following of predators behind the wildebeest migration which had exploded since the end of cattle ranching in 1938: "Boyd saw three lion cubs, two to three months old on the Mshabene dry riverbed. One he caught and then let go. There was also spoor of a male. The next day he saw eight lions and another nine cubs. He also saw two lionesses each with four cubs in the Princess Alice Bush area, walking together with a very large lone male giraffe. Lions were more plentiful than on any previous trip but one and that was in 1940 and sightings included a pride of twelve including two lionesses with cubs, one almost full grown cub with a lioness, two males

Above: Recording the history of the Sabi Sand on the 50th anniversary of the arrival of Charles Varty and Frank Unger – the first private landowners – Madeleine Varty wrote: "The founders of the Sabi Sand were prepared to finance the preservation of game areas so they could hunt. It may seem paradoxical, but I think it is valid to say that, but for hunting, it is unlikely that there would be a Sabi Sand today."

Left: Sparta abounded with lions in the 50s.

Above, Madeleine and Boyd Varty on their farm Sparta; and below, with their three children on the rocks of the Sand river.

Right: In the autumn of 1953 Maidie Varty wrote in her Sparta Game Book: "Impala were scarce but wildebeest and zebra had had a good calving season. Giraffe spoor seen, kudu normal. Waterbuck, small game and warthog had increased. We saw plenty of jackals, a pride of lions and eight cheetah. Hyena scarcer. The Sand river was running extremely high." On their next trip the bush was very thick after the late rains and offered good concealment for kudu and waterbuck. Boyd tracked leopard spoor and saw the cat emerge on the opposite bank of the river. Sparta was a wild paradise.

and a female with well grown cubs. Hyena and jackal were extremely numerous and no less than 15 cheetah were living on Sparta. Leopard were heard in the reedbed. One morning, after rain, the spoor of 31 hyena were counted, also eight cheetah and four lion. Baboons were plentiful and were killing young impala and duiker. Wild dog were seen chasing impala on the river. Five sable cows and one bull were sighted on the Mshabene and a wildebeest herd with calves. Kudu were more numerous than they had been for ten years. There was evidence of duiker, steenbuck and ostrich poaching and one zebra and a lion were found snared. No signs of crocodile this year."

After the war petrol was freely available and the roads improved making travel to the bushveld very much easier. Boyd, however, kept Sparta as wild and natural as possible. Only a few almost impassable roads were hacked out of the bush. When asked why his roads were so rough, Boyd would say: "So no one will come and visit me." "Boyd," says Madeleine, "was not really anti-social. He just loved the bushveld and the quiet and peace he found there."

On one occasion Madeleine, with two friends Beverley Hayward and John Hampton, were travelling from Johannesburg to Sparta when they got well and truly stuck up to their axles in the black turf along the Toulon/Newington road. They were not expected at camp and without any form of communication eventually had no option but to resign themselves to spending the night in the bush. Then, after sunset, they heard a steam engine approaching. Madeleine grabbed a pink nighty from her case and ran the 100 yards through the bush to the line waving it furiously at the driver who happily waved back and went on his way. But then the penny dropped. A woman on her own? In the dark? Miles and miles from anywhere? About 10 minutes later they heard the chug, chug, chug of the train reversing up the line to rescue them. They hitched a ride to Toulon but still had a long walk from the siding to Harry Kirkman's house, through an area Madeleine described as a lions' favourite playground.

The gun hut was one of Dave's earliest memories: "It was John's and my task to clean all the guns just before dark. Then when the lamps were lit we would check them by looking down the barrel into the bright lamp light. Only when all the guns were clean and back in the rack would we go down to the fire and serve drinks. Then we'd get our dinner and were sent off to bed.

"Some days were very long, starting well before dawn and ending long after sunset," said Dave. "We were usually woken at about four o'clock to go out in the freezing cold of a July winter morning. At least we had a mug of hot coffee. We would sit, dead still, listening for the roar of lion. One morning Dad made a mistake and woke us at twenty-past-two. He thought it was ten-past-four and had misread the clock. We sat there shivering in the freezing dark, waiting and waiting. After a long while Charz Brayshaw, a hunting companion, asked: 'When's the bloody sun going to rise?' But dawn was still a long way off!"

Dave remembers when he was about five and John eight: "We found a tree full of monkeys. By that time we had learnt to handle guns, but I was not very successful at holding aim with a steady hand. I rested my single-load BSA .22 calibre rifle on Winnis's shoulder and pulled off at least 50 rounds, missing every shot. Winnis then went to fetch more bullets while we remained at the scene intending to keep the monkeys up the tree. But once Winnis had left us, the monkeys climbed down and ran away. Even they seemed to respect his presence!"

The friendship that developed between the Varty family and Winnis Mathebula and many of his colleagues belonged to a past age, hardly recognisable in the South Africa of the 1980s and early 1990s. It was based on mutual respect, concern and trust and it is sad that South Africa's dominant political party for nearly 50 years should so skilfully have destroyed the elements on which relationships between black and white people could be built.

Winnis was not only teacher, guide and friend, he was a second father to Dave and John. "Our father had absolute trust in his ability to teach us and to look after us when we were in the bush," Dave recalls, "and when Winnis stopped and put two SSG cartridges into the breech of his shotgun and closed the barrel, we knew something was very, very close."

Twice Winnis nearly lost his life in the bush. The first incident occurred while he was cutting reeds along the banks of the Sand river. An old belligerent buffalo came up behind him but because of the sound of the river Winnis did not hear him. The buffalo charged, his horns piercing Winnis's side, and he was hurled a considerable distance. Winnis tried to sham dead but the bull, undeceived, roared in for a second attack, tossing him again, this time into a thorn bush. Still conscious and displaying great presence of mind, Winnis pushed rags into his wounds to staunch the massive bleeding. Fortunately Winnis's wife was nearby and she was able to run for help. Weak from loss of blood, Winnis was rushed to hospital in Bushbuckridge, nearly 50 miles away. Unconscious for seven days, he fought for his life and eventually recovered.

Other near misses included his being run over by a tractor and then, when he was 80 years old, while sitting around the village campfire at Londolozi he was attacked by a black mamba. According to Spook Sithole who was a chef at Londolozi for 25 years, Simeon was the first to be struck but, by an incredible stroke of luck, the mamba hit his belt and the venom trickled down his leg. The mamba then went for Winnis, biting him twice. But all the poison had drained from his fangs in that first strike and Winnis was unharmed. On another occasion, Spook relates: "When Winnis was sleeping at the entrance to his house the baboons apparently mistook his shiny black head for a pumpkin and tried to make off with it!" Winnis woke up fast with a severe gash in his scalp where one had bitten him. Once again the indestructible Winnis survived.

In 1959, after 26 years' service, Harry Kirkman resigned as a warden of the Kruger Park and to the delight of the community he returned to the Sabi Sand to sit down at the same campfire he had left in 1933. He had had a successful term of office and was loved by all who came in contact with him. He knew what was going on in the Park; one of his listening posts, according to Dave, was the Skukuza post office where the girls fed him all the gossip.

On one occasion Harry was tipped off that men manning the trains through the Sabi Sand were poaching. Blinded by the bright headlights of the locomotive the animals were an easy target. Harry set a trap and the crew were caught red-handed. The law was clear: if poachers were caught, not only were the weapons and the carcasses confiscated, but also the vehicle used. So Harry held the train while Ian Mackenzie, chairman of the Sabi Sand, phoned the Minister of Transport, Ben Schoeman, to advise him that his train had been confiscated! One can just imagine the retort. 'You can't be serious! You can't do that.' Eventually they struck a deal and until the track was pulled up, the railways maintained the surface of the road that runs alongside the line using fly-ash from the coal-burning steam engines.

With their .22's, John and Dave shot just about anything; doves, jackal, baboon, francolin, and when they were older and had bigger guns, lion, leopard and hyena. John's first gun, a 30.06, had a short stock and a muzzle breaker which reduced recoil and didn't bruise shoulders. John was only 12 when he shot a big black-maned lion at 60 metres. Dave shot his first, and only lion, when he was 15. He remembers: "Dad had two wishes for his sons, one that we would both go to university and, secondly, that we would each shoot a lion before he died. He had had rheumatic fever as a child and knew he had a weak heart. But, like Winnis, he was fearless and we thought, indestructible."

Dave and John had grown up in a society which believed that all predators should be treated as vermin. The established Kruger Park policy was to control carnivore so as to give the antelope a chance to recover from the devastations of commercial exploitation and disease. "Today when you have to pay hundreds of thousands of rands to stock a reserve, as we have at Phinda in KwaZulu/Natal where we did a massive restocking exercise, introducing both predators and their prey, you become more understanding of this practice," comments Dave. "It's not much fun paying R1000 for a kudu and the next day finding a heap of bones left by hyena.

"When we went out hunting we learnt to observe and to be disciplined. We also learnt the technique of the hunt, information that has never been recorded in text books. It was only when we stopped hunting and got into photography that we started to learn about animal behaviour." The science of sociobiology was in fact in its infancy and was not extensively studied as an academic subject until the 1970s.

The Sparta trackers were brilliant and had all been exceptional hunters: Winnis, Two-tone, Snotice. Dave and John hunted with them and learnt from these men. "When we went in after an animal with a gun our objective was to kill," Dave says. "But when we stopped shooting and started looking, we began to build a bank of information and started on a slow journey to a higher awareness in our relationship with wildlife. It was, however, beyond Winnis's understanding that when we moved from hunting to photography we should track a lion only to sit and gawk at it. He would shake his head at our foolishness.

Above: Learning to shoot was an important part of growing up in the bush.

Below: John shot a wildebeest in 1963 and that same season shot a big black-maned lion.

"With our high ethical code we thought we were 'conservationist' hunters – if there is such a thing. We always shot the lone wildebeest because we thought he was no longer good for breeding. In fact we were completely wrong. The lone wildebeest was the dominant male and later research has shown us that the females used to come through his territory. He was the prime breeding bull. Every year we shot this prime animal in the belief that he was the old throwout. It was much the same with lions. We always hunted the male lion with the biggest mane. Now we know that in shooting the dominant male, we completely upset the territories of lions. It was his job to control the area and to ensure the genetic superiority of his species. We discovered that shooting a female hyena would lead to the complete collapse of the clan; the same with wild dogs. We were brought up to believe that these animals were vermin. This attitude did not change until the late 1960s. We simply did not know how destructive we were. But things were changing, and we did not know why. In fact there were people taking decisions that were to prove more destructive than all the sportsmen's guns and all the poachers' snares put together."

After the recognition by the Transvaal Provincial Administration of Sabi Sand Wildtuin as a private game reserve in 1962, there was a distinct tailing off of hunting. Thereafter, apart from impala which had increased in numbers dramatically and were being culled, only a few lions and other predators were shot.

Dave believes that there has been a slow but relentless change in the habitat since the earliest days when man invaded the bushveld. Cattle ranching, which never permitted the land to rest, had denuded the grasslands and left a legacy of soil erosion. From 1938 until the erection of the Kruger Park fence in 1960, there was a huge buildup in the wildebeest population which favoured the drier, short grass conditions. The large numbers of these animals further de-nuded the grasslands and erosion continued unchecked. The sedentary, selective feeders were unable to cope with the fierce competition for grazing. Waterbuck which had been seen in herds of 70 in the 1920s started to disappear a long time before the fence was erected in 1960; as did the sable, roan and reedbuck which were, in effect, eaten out of house and home by the massive wildebeest population. At the same time the non-selective feeders and the browsers such as buffalo, kudu, and impala began to increase in numbers.

The early evidence of change is all set out in Madeleine's journal. At the beginning of 1960 she wrote: "This is the last year without the benefit or draw-back of fences. The Kruger National Park fence is proceeding apace and so is that around the Sabi Sand. It will be interesting to see what effect the fences will have. The most conspicuous need, I should imagine, is for more water points apart from the Sand river." An ominous comment.

The ostensible intention of the Kruger Park fence was to control foot-and-mouth disease but the Sabi Sand community and many field people in the

Above: In 1964 Boyd had no choice but to shoot a rogue elephant. Spook Sithole heard the story from Winnis who was with Boyd on a walk to the big dam. "They came around a bush and the elephant charged," said Spook. "Winnis shouted to Boyd to shoot, otherwise they would have been crushed to death."

Opposite: Wildebeest, often killed by lion. Madeleine wrote of the morning in 1951 when Boyd and Winnis with two friends, John Ferguson and Norman Trundell, came across jackals feeding on a wildebeest killed during the night by lions: "Norman suggested that they climb two nearby trees and await results. Within a short while a lioness appeared. When she was about 100 yards out a wildebeest got wind of her and ran off. She made a half-hearted attempt to chase him and then approached again until she stood under Norman's tree. The dis-tance between his feet and her head was a matter of two metres. Then as though an electric shock passed through her (perhaps it was the sudden whiff of Winnis's shoes left under the tree) she pricked up her ears, dropped her head and slunk silently off into the thorn scrub."

John and Dave recall patrolling the fence with Harry Kirkman in the 60s: "We saw about 450 buffalo on the Kruger Park side of the fence, all with their noses towards the Sand river which was inaccessible to them. Harry cut the barbed-wire fence and then ran into the park and chased the buffalo into the Sabi Sand, repairing the fence behind him. That's how the Sabi Sand got its buffalo."

There was no doubt that the fence, which formed a barrier between the Kruger National Park and the Sabi Sand for 33 years, spelt disaster. Although it was put up in the name of veterinary protection, it would appear that it was based more on a polarising political ideology than on any conservation principles. It took no account of geo-ecological features such as watersheds and river systems and not only restricted the movement of mobile species towards their traditional grazing grounds, but also cut them off from the Sand river. As soon as the fence was closed wildebeest and zebra had no option but to turn back on habitat that had already been grazed. This started a vicious cycle of degradation that was to spin out of control. The result was an ecological disaster and the decimation of the western population of wildebeest.

Left: An immature carmine bee-eater on the barbed-wire Kruger Park fence. Right: Wildebeest and buffalo.

Above: *Colotis antevippe*, red tip; *Acraea neobule*, wandering donkey Acraea; *Danaus chrysippus aegyptius*, African monarch; *Byblia anvatara acheloia*, common joker; and *Acraea anemosa*, broad-bordered Acraea.

From the top: Ghosts of marula pips eaten by unknown grubs. An egg case left by mantid hatchlings. A piece of quartz, possibly carrying minute traces of gold which has been found in the Sand river, but only in insignificant quantities.

Kruger Park, knew the effect that this 'Berlin Wall of Conservation', as Dave calls it, would have on game populations. Dave remembers Harry Kirkman telling him that, when the decision was taken to put up the fence, he made a deal with the veterinary department which promised that the Park would not fence the Sabi Sand out if the Sabi Sand's western border was fenced before their team got to the Sand river. Perhaps they had no intention – or no authority – to change this instruction. However, they made sure that their promise was void by putting three fencing crews onto the Kruger Park's western border, and beating Harry's crew, despite the fact that they fenced as hard as they could go.

In an attempt to provide a source of water for the animals after the fence had cut them off from the Sand river, boreholes were sunk but no account was taken of the fact that in times of drought animals do not die of thirst, they die of starvation. In addition, in the drought years immediately after the fence was erected the waterholes, which tapped underground systems and lowered the water-table, further accelerated the drying out of the habitat. Around every artificial water point star degradation developed, leading eventually to massive sheet erosion. The result was that animals died of starvation in their thousands. During the next few years in the western section of the Kruger National Park an estimated 18 000 wildebeest died. To alleviate their suffering over 3000 wildebeest were shot by KNP officers and by 1979 the western population had declined to 752. Thirty-five years later this western population has still not recovered.

In their place came impala which, because they are highly adaptable, thrive on down-graded habitat. They can graze and they can browse. But as the impala increased, the degradation worsened and the land's ability to withstand droughts weakened. The land was now caught in a vicious cycle of advancing desertification – an ugly word for an ugly process. Fundamentally the productivity of the land had been weakened reducing the biodiversity and favouring only those animals which could tolerate the changed conditions.

Madeleine's journal noted the increase in the wildebeest population until the fence was closed, and at the same time the dwindling numbers of some species and the disappearance of others. In 1960 she wrote: "There are more wildebeest and zebra than have been seen for many years. Twenty-five giraffe were seen in two days while lions were seen three times in one day. This included a pride of 11 in the river near Winnis's old home. But roan, tsessebe, sable, reedbuck and ostrich are gone and wild dog and cheetah rare."

Each year thereafter the comments in Madeleine's journal record their increasing concern for the diminishing numbers of animals. In 1962, the year after the fence was closed, her entry read: "The river was at its lowest level ever for the end of summer. Only two sable bulls seen." (They were the last recorded sightings of sable on Sparta.) Two years later she recorded that the new dam was holding water well and had been patronised by giraffe and elephants. They had seen signs of buffalo. Otherwise game was scarce and kudu, which had earlier been so plentiful, had disappeared while lions were not heard except at a very great distance.

In 1965 Madeleine noted the complete change in the species mix and in their numbers; kudu and impala were plentiful while wildebeest and giraffe were scarce. Only one waterbuck and one bushbuck were seen. Two years later game was even more scarce and very scattered. Wildebeest and zebra had diminished and grazing was in a poor condition. Predators had virtually disappeared. Rain was badly needed and the dams were dry. The problem of water had crept up on them almost unnoticed. Even after the disastrous western veterinary fence was taken down in 1994, the water resource remains a serious threat to the future of the Kruger National Park and the private game reserves.

The eastern Transvaal had always been subject to extraordinarily haphazard rainfall patterns. Some years there was drought, some years flood. As far back as the 1870s Alfred Aylward wrote: "The streams and waters in the northeast of the Transvaal are undoubtedly diminishing in volume and the dry seasons longer and drier." The erratic rainfall pattern was certainly no 20th century phenomenon and there is one solution: that is to maximise the effective rainfall by preventing run-off.

Photographs in the Varty archives clearly show that at the time of Charles's arrival at Sparta in 1926, the area was open grassland with occasional large trees dotted here and there. A few copses of scrub bush did occur, but the terrain was mostly open savannah. John remembers the Sand river flowing so high during summer that for months at a time they were unable to make a crossing and the water was always clear and sparkling. The area since then has undergone a major drying-out process. To try and cope, Boyd built two dams where he remembered in earlier years there had been vleis or marshy ground where game had come down to drink. But in 1966 Madeleine wrote: "The top dam is empty, and the river very low. The second dam had water but would be dry by the end of August." In 1968 both dams were dry. A few years later, for the first time in living memory, the great Sand river stopped flowing.

"My father," said Dave, "was becoming more and more concerned about the diminishing species and about the condition of the veld. He had always been a great, but fair hunter. But he recognised that the sunset of hunting had arrived and a new era of conservation had to begin."

In August 1969 Boyd went on a guineafowl shoot in the northern Transvaal. He arranged for Dave to spend the first week of his school holidays at Sparta with a friend – such was the trust he had in his 15-year-old son. He planned to join Dave at the end of the week. John had matriculated the previous year and was spending a year of compulsory military service in the South African Air Force. Dave remembers Harry Kirkman arriving at Sparta: "I saw Harry Kirkman

Above and below: As the bushveld dried out, animals, with the exception of impala, became more and more scarce. Giraffe were low and sable disappeared altogether.

from a distance, and knew immediately there was something very, very wrong. He told me my father had had a heart attack and had died that day. It was the 30th August. It was the end of the world for us. I cannot imagine that for the rest of my life I will ever again have to face such a devastating moment."

Madeleine later added a postscript to her journal – it was her last entry. It read: "This was the end of our bushveld story. Boyd died on 30th August 1969. We had had Sparta camps together for 27 years." Behind those words was so much love and sadness.

"Our father taught us everything," Dave said. "He taught us to love and to care. Every single day that we had spent on Sparta had been extraordinary. There had been wild days, days filled with fun and laughter, but we had been learning all the time about animals and about people. Sparta had taught us about life itself. If those years had been a gift from our father, it was a gift that involved a commitment." John, Dave, and most of all, Madeleine, were ready to make that commitment.

Many years later Madeleine returned to Sparta, to a special place on the Sand river that Boyd loved above all others. It was his refuge, his den. A memorial plaque there reads:

In memory of
BOYD VARTY
11 March 1914 – 30 August 1969
He loved the bushveld.

Left: The early morning bushveld mist on Sparta clears to reveal a leopard in a marula tree.

HARD TIMES

When the planet herself sings to us in our dreams
will we be able to wake ourselves and act?
— *Gary Lawless.*

UR WORLD had been turned up-side-down," recalls Dave. "But out of that moment of devastating sadness, came great opportunity. We were on the threshold of a journey of learning and excitement beyond anything we could have dreamt of or could even comprehend at the time."

Until that moment their thrills and excitement had revolved around hunting dangerous animals on Sparta and an abiding love of the game of cricket. Back home in Johannesburg Boyd had been passionate about the sport and had passed on his enthusiasm to his sons. Every spare moment was spent at the Wanderers Club. "John had played for South African Schools three years running and was moving up the ranks of the provincial teams," said Dave. "Then came the Basil d'Oliviera affair and South Africa began its long road to sporting isolation. (Basil d'Oliviera, a coloured cricketer from South Africa, was refused re-entry to South Africa as a member of the MCC team.) Now all thoughts of playing county and international cricket and of having fun at Sparta faded into the mist. The guns and cricket bats were packed away and John and Dave left adolescence behind and grew up overnight.

"My mother was faced with the cost of university education for three children. My sister, Claudia, was already at Stellenbosch University in the Cape. John was to start university the following year and I planned to join him studying for a B.Com. degree when I matriculated," said Dave.

"That year is well remembered in South Africa for another reason. In 1969 the bottom fell out of the share market. The value of the investments my father had left were halved. But death duties had been calculated at the date of death. Our trustees advised our mother to dispose of her non-income-earning assets so that she could pay the estate duties and be left with a reasonably comfortable income and sufficient funds for our education. The logical decision was to keep her shares and sell Sparta and there was in fact a very handsome offer on the table. However there was another asset, a mining materials business, which our father had built up. With the most valuable advice and guidance of her brother-in-law, Arthur Thomas, that business continued successfully for another six years and obviated the need to sell Sparta – which later became Londolozi.

"I don't think the question of selling Sparta was ever an issue. It would have been like selling her arms. And, just as our father had handed us our first guns when we were only five years old with an incredible trust that we would follow his instructions implicitly, now our mother handed us the responsibility of taking care of Sparta. I was 15 and John was 18. She made it clear to John and me that she could not help us financially. There was enough for our board and lodging and our university fees, but there simply was nothing over for the development of any grand – or even small – ideas we might have for Sparta.

"Our mother had turned her back on financial wealth and security and,

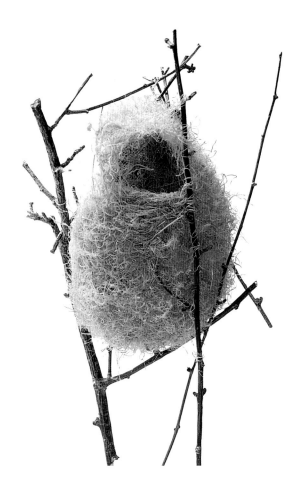

Above: A beautiful nest made by a mouse and a nest made by a black cuckooshrike, *Campephaga flava*.

Left: Cape buffalo of the eastern Transvaal almost disappeared with the epidemics of rinderpest in 1896 and foot-and-mouth disease in 1938. However, over the years their numbers increased and they have been successfully harvested on a sustainable basis for over 30 years.

Hadeda ibis, *Bostrychia hagedash*.

Lizard buzzard,
Kaupifalco monogrammicus.

Bateleur, *Terathopius ecaudatus*.

Jackal buzzard, *Buteo rufofuscus*.

Gymnogene, *Polyboroides typus*.

Scale in cm.

with a generosity we will never find again, she gave us the opportunity and the means to be in the driving seat of our lives and our careers. The following year I wrote my matric and in 1971 I joined John at university in Johannesburg. That year Shan Watson came into our lives. And I found the Watson family.

"She was just a little schoolgirl when I met her," Dave says with a wry smile. "Let's get one thing straight, I wasn't interested." He was 17 and a university student, with wide-set blue eyes and already showing promise of the rugged good looks that both brothers would develop in their 20s. Shan was 15 and dressed in bobby socks and a Panama hat. But in her Dave had found a friend and a companion who would slowly fill the void in his life, share his dreams and work tirelessly by his side.

Shan may have still been at school but she was no gawky kid. With her long dark hair falling almost to her waist, her graceful, athletic figure and ready smile, she was already an attractive young woman. She also had a sensitive nature and, below the surface, a firm determination that she would direct the course of her life. Dave had met his match! Shan was soon aware that Dave was different from many of her other boyfriends. Shan takes up the story: "We met while on holiday at Queensbury on the coast near East London where we shared a fishing shack with the Williams and Patmore families. That holiday Dave came down with his friend, Ralph Patmore. I noticed that Dave often went off by himself walking along the beach very early in the morning." A few months later, Dave found himself without a 'chick' and invited Shan to the cinema. It was not long before he was talking about his father and about Sparta – and attempting to persuade her parents to allow her to visit Sparta with him. By that time Dave was virtually a family member.

"My mother never left our house for almost the first year after dad's death," Dave recalls. So when Madeleine had, at the insistence of good friends in England, gone to stay with them, Dave spent more and more time with the Watsons, finding himself welcomed by the entire family. "On one occasion after my mother had returned from her overseas trip I had to call her to say I was going to be home late from the Watsons because Shan's old man wouldn't let me get away!" Shan says: "With four daughters, dad was incredibly strict, but with Dave he developed a wonderful relationship and there was an instant trust." Brian Watson was the exact opposite from Dave. Dave neither drank nor smoked and at that time of his life he was very introspective. "My dad was gregarious, outgoing, very social and enjoyed a drink, a smoke, dancing and fun. He was the life and soul of a party."

Breaking all the rules of society at the time, it was not long before Dave would collect his 16-year-old girlfriend from Maryvale Convent and together with Gavin and Marilyn Joyce, 'who were amongst our earliest visitors and became great friends,' would be off to the bush as often as they could on Friday afternoons, returning on Sundays. Neither Dave nor Shan had their own transport so they were always dependent on a guest to drive them. "For R3 a day you could come to Sparta," Dave recalls. "You had to bring your own food and drink, even your own bedding and if you had a Land Rover and musical instruments, so much the better. We had to cadge a lift from our first guests, two girls, an Australian and a South African, who brought plenty of gin and tonics and not much else. It was a great weekend but the catering was lousy."

At the end of 1973 John decided that enough was enough. He hated city life. He had had enough of exams and whether he passed or not he was going to live at Sparta and start a safari business. "John was always very fiery," Dave says. "He picked up a Zulu dictionary, opened it and said: 'What's this, Londolozi – protector of all living things. That sounds O.K.' And so we had the name. It had taken a few minutes, if that."

There were many reasons why John and Dave decided to turn their essentially hunting camp into a photographic safari business. From 1962 when the Sabi Sand received official recognition as a private game reserve, hunting was restricted in the area. Soon after that Urban Campbell, Wac's eldest son, started the first photographic safari operation in the Sabi Sand at Mala Mala, a camp that was renowned during the Wac Campbell years as a huntsmen's paradise. "Hunting became of less importance to my father in the final years of his life," Dave said. "He had come to the realisation that with the political demands on land, wildlife must pay in another way."

Today Dave admits that although he improved somewhat from his first attempts at shooting monkeys, he could never shoot straight. "I continued to be clumsy and infinitely preferred to spend a day in the bush listening to the marvellous tales that Winnis could relate. Descending from a nation of famed raconteurs, Winnis was one of the best. He would enthral us with his stories.

"After our father died, for both John and me the switch from hunters to conservationists was a natural extension to our Sparta existence. In a way our hunting techniques paved the way for photographic safaris but we were directed there by our growing awareness that the game was disappearing and something had to be done about it. The bushveld and its animals were our abiding passion and from the start we saw the safari business as a means to an end. We wanted to integrate our guests into our conservation endeavour. We thought we could put animals back into the Sabi Sand and they would stay there – how wrong we were!"

There was nothing small about John and Dave's ambitions. They decided to attack four different segments of the safari market in one go: advertising luxury and rough safaris, a trails camp and a canoe safari on the Sand river, which on its very first excursion ended literally on the rocks.

"We were going to conquer the entire safari market. We thought we'd

Top: Kudu, a species that was once hunted for its magnificent horns.

Above: White rhino disappeared from the Sand river area before the turn of the century and were only re-introduced into the Sabi Sand Wildtuin in the mid-60s. With good protection these animals have thrived ever since.

make millions of rands overnight," says Dave. "We had four huts and one rickety old Land Rover and we advertised our rough safari camp for 10 people. The concept of fitting ten people into four bedrooms and a single Land Rover never for a moment crossed our minds. In our naivety we made more mistakes more often than seems possible. We bought a water tank with our last cash resources and set it up on a tower we built from knobthorn poles. But our engineering skills were distinctly lacking. There we were, admiring our handiwork as the tank filled. Then just as our guests arrived the poles began to creak and sway under the increasing weight and the tank collapsed in a crumpled heap. No showers. No flushing toilets. It was back to the river. But we did get wonderful support from the owners of farms neighbouring Sparta.

"Tom Robson senior, a great friend of our father had, after several visits to Sparta, bought Othawa, a farm also on the Sand river. Tom had been on the guineafowl shoot when my dad died and he had made a promise to him that he would ensure that both John and I got our university degrees. We had arranged traversing rights over Othawa but when John tried to skip university Tom Robson threatened to cancel these rights. We had no choice. Somehow or other John had to write his final exams and start our business at the same time. I not only had to finish university, but I also had to do a year's military service.

"It was not long before we had a plan of action," Dave relates. "John went off to the bush with Howard Mackie who was a key person in the founding of Londolozi. I stayed in Johannesburg and did what I could for the business at this end. At the same time it was my job to ensure that both John and I qualified to write our final exams. That meant I had to make notes and coach John over weekends. At the end of the year we wrote our finals and we were down at Londolozi when we got the news on the two-way radio that we had both passed our exams for our B.Com. degrees. We will always be indebted to Tom Robson for honouring the promise to our father and taking a firm stand with us."

In 1973 another problem confronted owners of Sabi Sand farms. Out of the blue a letter was received from the Bantu Affairs Commission (bantu, the Zulu word for people):

"I have been directed to inform you that although the farms Exeter, Othawa, Wallingford, Ravenscourt, Alicecot and Castleton, district Pilgrims Rest, were excised from the Released Area a few years ago, consideration is now being given to the proposed inclusion of the farms in the Bantu Area, in order to obtain a meaningful consolidation of Lebowa and Gazankulu."

This was the first intimation that the government's iniquitous policy of decentralisation under which large communities were forcibly removed to reservations, irrespective of whether they wanted to move or not, would directly affect the Sabi Sand. Already suffering from the effects of the fence, Sabi Sand

In the 1970s young men from Boy's Town (top) and sponsored by the Wilderness Education Trust (above) had a great time with John – whether their Land Rover broke down or not! Even then John's easy ability to communicate with young people had become evident.

Left: The Sand river in the early morning is a hive of activity. The call of a fish eagle echoes across the water, kingfishers swoop on unsuspecting fish, a green-backed heron waits patiently in the shadows and oxpeckers take their chance grooming hippos in shallow pools.

Three different butterflies of the family Papilionidae: The large striped swordtail, *Graphium antheus*; the citrus swallowtail or Christmas butterfly, *Papilio demodocus* and the green-banded swallowtail, *Papilio nireus*.

was now to be halved in size – effectively a death sentence for the game reserve. Two of the farms which faced expropriation were part of the Mala Mala group, while another two, Othawa and Ravenscourt, were part of Londolozi's traversing area. The cause was taken up on behalf of the Sabi Sand owners by Ian Mackenzie, chairman of the Standard Bank group in South Africa. Largely as a result of his visit to the Prime Minister in Cape Town with Jaap Wilkens who owned the farm Dudley in the Sabi Sand, the proposal was dropped. If it had gone ahead, it would have spelt the end of the Sabi Sand reserve. Homeland development elsewhere has led to totally unproductive land denuded of vegetation by overgrazing. As Ian Mackenzie wrote in his letter to the Minister: "It would be a national tragedy if such an important resource were to be destroyed". He was right. Today the Sabi Sand generates over R100 million annually and provides employment directly for more than 1000 people and indirectly for many more. Of even greater significance, an irreplaceable biodiversity of wildlife would have been lost.

Although they had escaped on that occasion, it was a warning to absentee landlords who would be extremely vulnerable in the years ahead. Only in ecotourism, earning foreign exchange and creating jobs, would owners of land have an answer against expropriation.

Yet another problem loomed on the horizon. Londolozi was wedged between two vastly different political ideologies which were on a collision course. On the one side was the extreme right of the apartheid system, on the other, only 40 kilometres away from Londolozi as the crow flies, the growing communist threat in Moçambique was about to erupt into full-scale war. By 1980 some of the Sabi Sand owners were so concerned about bombs and rockets that they were using corrugated iron roofing instead of thatching to reduce the risk of fire. Refugees fleeing from the war zone more often than not crossed the narrow section of the Kruger Park directly opposite Londolozi. Many reached safety with hair-raising stories. Some did not arrive at all. It was a case of preferring the African lion to the Russian bear.

"In those early years when our cash flow was as erratic as the weather we never had enough food and were always hungry," Dave recalls. "Our standard diet was impala and putu." (A porridge made from ground maize.) "On one occasion in the early 70s we came around a corner and found lions on a wildebeest they had just killed. We were so hungry we chased off the lions and loaded the wildebeest onto the back of our jeep. It had been raining and under the heavy load the jeep just sank into the mud, really deep. We had no chance of getting out easily and the lions were very angry and probably just as hungry as we were. We had one gun and five bullets between us and no radio. It was getting dark and the lions were closing in on us. The one thing we did have was a knife. So we started cutting up the wildebeest and throwing chunks of meat

Two *Commelina* species belonging to the spiderwort family, Commelinaceae.

Lions attacked many refugees who walked across the Kruger Park to find friends, family and safety further west. Rosaline Ndlovu, who now works at Londolozi, was one of many women who fled with their children away from the conflict in Moçambique. Her husband and one child were killed but she managed to hide with her three remaining children in the mealie fields. When the sounds of the AK47's stopped she carried one child on her back and another in her arms right across the Kruger Park, facing lions and many other terrors until she reached the safety of Londolozi 13 years ago.

to the lions. Eventually they moved off and we could offload the jeep and dig our way out. I think some of the wildebeest was left for dinner.

"Transport was another huge problem. Eventually, by a stroke of luck we managed to buy a second Land Rover. It was exam time and John was in Johannesburg when we read an ad that a 1959 Series II Land Rover, the same as ours, was for sale at R450 – at 8th Avenue, Lower Houghton, just a few blocks from us. We were there like long dogs. Having two vehicles of the same model meant that we could cannibalise parts from one vehicle to keep the other operational. There was no money to carry a stock of spares.

"When we got to the house, an auction was going on and John bought the vehicle. The owner wanted payment immediately. John said 'Hang on, we'll get it!' John, used to giving orders to his younger brother, says: 'Dave, get me R450.' It's eight o'clock at night and I don't know where or how to get that kind of money. But John is not interested in my problem. He's a very fiery guy and with the seller demanding his money and another buyer offering R550, John is close to starting World War III. My mother is out so I go to my grandmother, Jessie Hellier. She's old and very deaf and used one of those horns. So now I have to shout at the top of my voice into her horn: 'Gran, Gran, GRAN, we need R450.'

"Gran is 92 but very with it and very practical: 'Why do you want R450?'

'To buy a Land Rover, Gran.'

'Why do you want a Land Rover, David?'

'Gran, we've got to have this Land Rover.'

"And all the time I'm picturing the scene around the corner with John about to use his fists. Eventually Gran goes to a little box, brings out a cheque book and starts to write out a cheque for us in a very shaky hand. I tear back, barge in waving my cheque. But this creates another problem. The seller doesn't want a cheque. He demands cash. After much haggling and with us telling him that our Gran is a zillionaire, which she wasn't, we got our Land Rover.

"We used to battle to keep our vehicles going. Certainly playing cricket every spare moment in Johannesburg and every holiday spent hunting had not equipped us to fix Land Rovers. Gavin Joyce, who often came to our rescue giving unstintingly of his time and knowledge, helped us rebuild a Land Rover in his parents' back garden in Johannesburg. John and Howard Mackie had the original hunting jeep and our second R450-Land Rover at Londolozi. We used to work on the vehicle several evenings a week and then be off to Londolozi on Friday afternoons, often with Shan. At that time she was still at school. Usually we'd get to Londolozi at about one or two in the morning and wake John up to find out what problems they had. More often than not it was a case of getting a vehicle on the road before dawn. Gavin and I would work through the night.

"At first light John would come out in his pyjamas and we would ask for another hour. John would then dress and Howard would emerge – in John's

Above: A specially patented brass ear-trumpet used by the hard-of-hearing.

Left above: Impala thrive in downgrading habitat and act as a 'buffer species' protecting vulnerable animals from over-predation. In the Sabi Sand impala are harvested for food. "When our visitors arrived we had to learn to improvise," says Dave. "Often our guests brought food that we didn't know how to prepare. On his wood stove, our cook Spook knew how to do an impala roast, impala kebab, impala stew or impala steak. An order for a rare grilled fillet completely upset his routine. We didn't have a grid to put on the fire, so we removed the grid from the front of the Land Rover to cook on and put it back on the vehicle the next morning!"

Left below: Wildebeest, weakened by the down-graded habitat and closed off from their natural migration routes, were particularly vulnerable to predation.

Above: Lion. Africa's most awesome predator. Standing 1.25 metres at the shoulder and having a mass of up to 235 kilograms, a male lion is at the top of the hierarchy of predators. Small wonder that they are daunting at full charge when they cover 100 metres in 4.2 seconds.

pyjamas – to see if he could help. Both clothes and Land Rovers were equally in short supply. Howard needed to know if both or only one vehicle was usable. If only one was in running order he would go off and 'sell' a walk to the guests.

"I remember one morning the jeep started up and – woosh! – the whole engine went up in flames. Howard, always cool under pressure and with a great sense of humour, took the guests for a walk and, displaying great confidence in our abilities, told us to catch up with him. Forty-five minutes later we did. Gavin had short-circuited the entire electrical system. He was a brilliant mechanic and I learnt everything I know about Land Rovers from him.

"Life in the bushveld was a comedy of errors. We had no radios so if we got stuck in the bush, we were out there for a long time. Once it was nearly midnight before we recovered a party. John had built a fire and had them all singing just as though it was part of the bush experience. In those days a good game drive was not measured by what you saw but whether you got back to camp without a breakdown."

Then there were times when they had to use their guns to get out of dangerous situations. John tells the story of when he was out collecting firewood with a group of young Shangaans. Totally unexpectedly, with the team spread out in all directions and concentrating on the job in hand, a pride of lions came in on the attack. John had no option but to shoot, first to protect one of the young men and then himself. He shot and killed one lion and wounded another. He then loaded up the men and attempted to get out of the trouble area as quickly as he could. He slammed the jeep into reverse and the gear stick snapped and came away in his hand! This gave him no choice but to reverse the jeep all the way back to camp, a distance of about four kilometres. By that time it was dark, his battery was virtually flat and he had to light matches to see where he was. The next day he went back to track and kill the wounded lion. It was like the hunting days revisited.

At the start of 1975 many things started to fall into place. For the first time John could concentrate fully on running Londolozi. Whenever he could, Dave helped but he still had to complete his military service. Shan took over from Lynn Ascham who had been handling reservations from her art gallery in the Carlton Centre and opened Londolozi's reservations office in the attic of her parents' home. "Dad had given me an Olivetti typewriter as a Christmas present. It was all we needed to get going, even if it didn't have an 'e'." She took a morning job as a veterinary assistant and worked in the afternoons promoting Londolozi and helping Dave and John. They paid her R75 a month. To supplement cash flow Shan also headed up fund-raising efforts: "We sold crayfish door-to-door to earn R25 a box in commission," says Shan. "And we sold impala skins from the culling of Sabi Sand stock. We spent our life lugging impala skins around shopping centres in Johannesburg and were covered in hair from top to toe."

The annual newsletters, with the 'e' still missing, and the minutes of the meetings between John and Dave make interesting reading. Before the start of 1975 they more than trebled their rates from R3 to R10 and they had no less than 18 advance bookings. At R10 per night they could earn R80 a day at full capacity and they were planning a semi-luxury camp for another 14 people which they would market at R20 a day taking their potential turnover to R360. Twenty-one years later, in 1996, Londolozi has a capacity of 48 beds at its three camps, generating up to R60 000 a day and giving employment directly to 150 people and indirectly to many more.

Not all their early safaris were successful. Their first luxury safari was a disaster from beginning to end. It had rained the whole week and the neighbouring airstrip was so saturated that the planes, which probably should never have landed, came in looking like motor boats. The roads were under water. It never stopped raining. They got stuck. They got lost on a neighbouring farm over which they had just gained traversing rights. There were washaways. And after 11 hours of driving they had not seen a single animal. Their guests never reached their luxury accommodation and to cap it all a plague of stinkbugs disrupted dinner which consisted of as tough a leg of impala as you could ever find. At the end of two days of sheer misery the guests were only too pleased to get away. So much for luxury! Madeleine Varty made them refund the entire R700 they had taken for the 10 guests' two-day adventure.

But money had always been only a means to an end for both John and Dave. What was particularly extraordinary about the two brothers with such widely different temperaments, was that they thought so much alike. The Shangaan people first nicknamed John, 'Tilu', meaning 'thunder and lightning' but later gave him the name 'Makhokhwana' – 'the man with the crooked arm' – which described his way of walking with his one arm bent. Dave earned the nickname 'Machelana' – 'one who talks incessantly'.

One of John's friends, Nombolo Ndluli, who had been on Stevenson-Hamilton's staff in the early days of the Kruger Park once told John: "You are two people. You and your brother are like one, but you have two heads and you can be in two places at one time. You're very lucky." John relates just what a wise old man he was: "Nombolo asked me why I had such long hair when most white men wore their hair close-cropped. I replied that in winter it's cold and my hair keeps me warm. He smiled, said that I was clever and then asked me why I didn't cut my hair in summer. I smiled back. On another occasion I asked Nombolo why, in his day, Shangaan people never stole anything and today the youngsters sometimes steal. Nombolo said it was all the white man's fault. He invented clothing with pockets, so that when someone steals, he can hide the object in his pockets, whereas his tribal attire never had pockets and the stolen object would be seen in his hand.

Spring in the bushveld is when the first rains fall, when the rivers start to flow and food is plentiful. This is also the season when animals drop their young. An impala looks decidedly bedraggled after a rainstorm, while a zebra foal takes shelter next to its mother.

Above and opposite: In the early 70s leopard were rarely seen on Londolozi and cheetah were in danger of disappearing altogether. Ross Parry-Davies suggested the formation of the Londolozi Game Trust to raise the funds to pay for the purchase and relocation of cheetah and many other species to Londolozi. This was to lead to an understanding that it was necessary first to address the cause of the disappearance of these species.

Next pages: Lions once so prolific in the area disappeared with the game.

"Londolozi safaris," John believes, "were based on the hunting ethic of tracking, walking and of finding animals. The only difference was that instead of shooting them we used our hunting skills to produce a leopard or a lion for our guests to photograph. You could say that our hunting experience is one of the reasons why Londolozi has become renowned for its sightings of wildlife and particularly leopards. To this day we have tracking units that go out every day in search of these elusive cats."

In 1975 John and Dave were becoming seriously concerned about the fall-off in species and in the numbers of animals they were seeing. Ross Parry-Davies, chairman of the geotechnical division of LTA (one of South Africa's leading construction companies) had visited Londolozi as a guest and had been impressed with the drive and enthusiasm of the Varty boys. He was to become not only a friend but also a self-appointed engineering consultant to Londolozi. With a Ph.D. in civil engineering they could hardly have done better. While he was there five cheetah got out of the Sabi Sand reserve and because they were not protected in the neighbouring homeland they had been shot by government officials. John was disconsolate. The cheetah population was now reduced to eight. Ross suggested that cheetah should be put back into the reserve. The problem for them, as with everything else they wanted to do, was simply no money. With Ross at the helm, the outcome was the forming of the Londolozi Game Trust with an initial launch in Johannesburg that raised R2500, enough to bring five cheetah from South West Africa to the Sabi Sand. Ross Parry-Davies, Ian Mackenzie, Craig Troeberg, a partner in a leading firm of chartered accountants, Tom Robson owner of Othawa, together with Dave and John, made up the board of trustees.

The Trust was intended to relocate animals from many parts of Africa as well as cheetah from South West Africa. They planned to relocate leopard from north-west Transvaal where they were often shot or trapped to prevent stock losses; sable, tsessebe and roan from war-torn Rhodesia; elephants from the Kruger Park where about 300 of these magnificent animals were being culled annually; and nyala from an overstocked Ndumu Game Reserve in KwaZulu/Natal. Initially it was intended to bring the animals into the Sabi Sand.

Later the project developed to encompass a much wider territory and the Trust helped stock the Pilanesberg Game Reserve at Sun City to the north-west of Johannesburg. After nearly a decade the Trust was closed. John and Dave felt that donations were not sustainable in the long term and that "we wanted to demonstrate that wildlife could stand up against industry, mining and agriculture as a profitable business."

The Trust developed on two levels. On the one hand Dave and John brought in captains of industry, international superstars and future political leaders to support their cause. On the other, Shan had a band of 11-year-old

Top: Tina Turner visited Londolozi and saw the sables relocated from a war-torn Rhodesia in the 70s.

Above and opposite: Irish folk-singer Chris de Burgh was so impressed with the elephant relocation programme that he staged an extra show in Johannesburg during his South African tour, with all proceeds donated to the Londolozi Game Trust.

boys helping her. "The cheetah project caught the imagination of a marvellous group of schoolboys," recalls Shan. "We used to go around from door-to-door on bicycles selling raffle tickets. Eventually we raised R15 000. The project sparked a lifelong passion for wildlife among the boys. Hugh Stroud went on to write a thesis on cheetah at the age of 15."

John and Dave found a wonderful ally in Spike Milligan, famous for his hilarious participation in BBC's Goon Show. He did all he could to help their fund raising efforts. Through Spike, Peter Sellers 'bought' an elephant. So did Paul and Linda McCartney, the Bee Gees and Elton John. Peter Sellers said he would like to name 'his' elephant Satchitananda.

The first money they raised was used to buy cheetah from South West Africa and transfer them to Johannesburg where they appeared in TV shows before they were set free at Londolozi. "Well," Dave says, "the cheetah took one look at our thick bush and turned tail and ran. They went looking for open savannah country which they found on the basalt plains of central Kruger Park where the cattle impact had been less. They had been fitted with collars so we were able to track them. We had made the same mistake as everyone else. We were looking at animals and not at habitat. We had the same result with our sables. We brought 40 sables in from Rhodesia. But sables are selective, high water-table feeders which survive on grasslands which had all but disappeared from Londolozi. They were released – and seen no more in the Sabi Sand.

"We had more success with our next project," recalls Dave. "Twenty-eight years ago the Kruger National Park had decided that its elephant population should be limited to 7500. There is no apparent reason how this figure was reached, but from then on until 1996 about 300 of these animals were culled every year. In 1976 we approached Dr. Tol Pienaar of the Kruger National Park. He was adamant that it would be impossible to move elephants outside the park because 'it had been proved that elephants carried the foot-and-mouth virus'. He was so convinced that we would never get permission to take the elephants across the fence, that he agreed that if we got approval from the veterinary authorities, he would let us have them. A few months later there was a change in senior staff in the veterinary department and we got the green light to set up the first elephant relocation operation."

All that Dave and John proposed was literally to take elephants across the fence which arbitrarily split their home range. The trauma that the elephants were subjected to should have been unnecessary and it is doubtful if it was of any advantage to limit the elephant population to 7500. "Today the KNP staff are world leaders in elephant relocation," says Dave. "They are an extremely professional team and make it look as easy as frying an egg. But this was the very first elephant relocation exercise and the eggs got scrambled!"

The first day they went in to catch elephants was a disaster. They had

decided that they would take three youngsters, darting them with the morphine-based capture drug M99, crating them and then transferring them by road to the Sabi Sand. "First of all," Dave says, "it took too long to locate our elephants so that by the time the three were darted the temperature was around 42° centigrade, much too hot for elephants in a drugged state. Secondly, in our inexperience, from the air we misjudged the size of the animals we darted. Then it was discovered that one of the darts had malfunctioned. We should have ignored that calf, instead we wasted more time redarting the same animal. Dr. Dave Meltzer, the veterinary surgeon, injected her with the antidote M285 and the calf revived completely in three short minutes. Quickly realising that the situation was far from normal, she was only persuaded to enter the crate with the assistance of about 40 Shangaan men hauling with all their strength on the end of a rope. Then we found we had made yet another mistake. The crate had been made to relocate sables and was a very tight fit. By this time the calf, about two metres at the shoulder, was fully awake. She took one deep breath and the crate burst open as though it had been made of boxwood. Suddenly, with two tons of very alert and annoyed baby elephant at one end, the rope took on a life of its own. And from one second tugging with all their might, the next moment 40 men literally abandoned stations and scattered in all directions. The last we saw of her was as she trotted off into the bush screaming in juvenile rage."

Meanwhile they had a very worried Dave Meltzer. The other two elephants had suffered from the heat and even though the team did all they could, the M285 failed to revive them. Overnight they strengthened the crates, putting gum poles down the sides and the next day they started earlier and worked faster. They knew the elephants could not handle heat and before 7.30am the animals were on their way through the Kruger Park to Londolozi by courtesy of Cargo Motor's Unimogs lent to them for the occasion. They even got caught speeding on their way but the elephants arrived in good shape.

Soon after that, through the efforts of their American Trust agent Tedd Schorman, John and Dave decided to try and persuade the director of ABC's 'American Sportsmen' series to support and participate in an elephant relocation operation. John recalls the scene: "John Wilcox was a very busy man and not terribly impressed with these two khaki-clad South Africans. In between taking calls, he let us know that he was not interested. Eventually I decided I would grab his attention but in my anxiety I got tongue-tied: 'We'll dart helicopters from elephant,' I said. That stopped him in his tracks. He replaced the phone and said 'Say that again!' I quickly corrected myself and added some New York salesmanship: 'I mean we'll dart elephants and then sling them under the chopper to transport them'. 'You can do that?' yelled the producer. 'O.K. we'll do it!' Now the ball was in my court and I wondered how the hell we were going to get the elephants hoisted under a chopper.

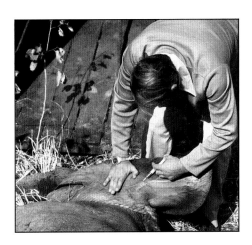

Above: Seconds before the antidote was administered and all hell broke loose, the relocation team manoeuvred the baby elephant into position to get her into the all-too-flimsy crate.

Left: About 300 Kruger Park elephants were culled each year to maintain their numbers at 7500 – a practice only discontinued in 1996. But in 1979 for the first time elephants were being saved from culling by being darted and relocated to new areas.

Altogether 11 young elephants were re-located to Londolozi where they were kept in a boma for several weeks. Each displayed a different emotion. Some were angry, some bewildered, two were terrified and literally clung to each other for protection. "Later we found it necessary to bring in a matriarch to help settle the youngsters,"

John says. "But that's how Londolozi got the nucleus of its breeding herd and the whole concept of elephant relocation was set in motion. I don't think there is any reason to cull elephants as long as there are places where they can live. The KNP has refined its technique and can now move mature elephants anywhere in the world."

"With that ABC was on its way to Londolozi to film the capture and relocation of our elephants," John said. "They agreed to fund the entire project. It was a highly complex shoot. The plan was to fly Cheryl Tiegs, the world's highest-paid model, with Ben Abruzzo, over the bushveld in a hot-air balloon during the darting of the elephants. The previous year Abruzzo had hit headlines when he made the first hot-air balloon transatlantic crossing."

Dave says he could never forget the scene: "Hot-air balloons, fleets of choppers, Land Rovers, ground crews, observers and hangers-on. There we were. All ready to go. The elephants had been located. The cameras ready to roll. Peter Johnson had set up a remote controlled camera on the helicopter. All eyes were on Ben Pretorius, the Kruger Park section ranger, a marvellous, dedicated man. He opened his medical box and turned white. He had left the M99 drug behind in Skukuza – 40 kilometres away. 'Die oomblik was te groot!' (It was the most embarrassing moment!)

"Ben turns to me and says: 'Dave, I haven't got the drugs! I forgot them!' Now it's not just the air temperature that is rising. Wilcox explodes. The tension is terrible and there is nothing we can do. We put Ben on a chopper, but it was too late and too hot to dart any elephants later that day. We just about got fried! The next day it all went like clockwork. We caught the little elephants and slung them under the chopper, flew them around so that the film crews could get their shots, and transported them to Londolozi. The KNP capture team was marvellous."

At that time the Trust also wanted to move elephants to Sun City's Pilanesberg Game Reserve. "They could take 150 elephants," said Dave. His statement was taken up by Cheryl Tiegs who shortly after her return to the U.S. began to set up a fund-raising gala evening at Studio 54, a famous night club in New York. The evening was to be hosted by Cheryl Tiegs, Peter Beard her boyfriend, and Fleetwood Mac. "We were to get the entrance monies for one night," Dave says. "There was a magnificent invitation to 'save an elephant' and, of course it was a spectacular evening. In the end we raised $69 000. The downside was that in true New York fashion the bill for the evening was $67 000!"

THE QUEST FOR SOLUTIONS

The first grass appeared 60 million years ago —
a revolution that was to change the world
with a slender green weapon that could be bitten
and continue growing. — *Creina Bond*.

L ONDOLOZI WAS GROWING UP FAST. "By 1975 we had started our own catering – after our self-catering guests had left us with 120 flora margarines and 60 packets of rusks," recalls Dave. "We had given up on the unequal struggle of trying to keep drop toilets hygienic at temperatures around 40°, and installed flush toilets, hot and cold showers and a bath. We built up from one rickety old Land Rover to two. From four mud huts to semi-luxury accommodation and a dining room with a roof. From R3 a day to R35. And all the time we were finding ourselves with less and less money. Our bank account went from a credit of R62.11 to an overdraft of over R20 000, and we were to stay in the red for a long time."

Just one of the many problems was that Londolozi was attracting more and more visitors to see fewer and fewer animals and the Vartys didn't know why. The sable, tsessebe, roan, reedbuck and ostrich had disappeared, the cheetah had run away, waterbuck populations were going down but impala were prolific. What was happening was that all the grassland or high water-table selective feeders were declining while species which favoured degrading bush habitat were on the increase.

The fence cutting off the Sabi Sand from the Kruger National Park had caused havoc. According to Ian Whyte, a biologist at the KNP, "the area utilized during the seasonal migratory movements of the wildebeest and zebra had been cut roughly in half with disastrous long-term results." On the Sabi Sand side, what game there was, was now concentrated into a relatively small area of 570 square kilometres. Animals such as wildebeest and zebra, whose mobility was their success, were unable to move beyond the fence in search of food. Game records kept by the Sabi Sand show that during the 1960s decade of drought, between 62 percent and 77 percent of the mortality of impala, wildebeest and zebra was as a result of starvation. And when the antelope disappeared so did the predators.

That wasn't all the damage, as Dave and John were later to discover.

As early as 1983 Dave and John had presented a document to the South African government's President's Council, suggesting linking together the Sabi Sand, Timbavati and Manyeleti reserves on the western border of the Kruger National Park and removing all game fences between these parks. When John tried to persuade the authorities that the parks were ecologically linked to a system that ran from the foothills of the Drakensberg to the park itself and they had to look at the entire picture, he found himself in a short but futile argument.

"Mr. Varty," said the chairman, "that area is part of the homelands and is ruled by the Shangaan people."

"No," said John utilising all the self-restraint he was capable of: "Nature's forces rule the rivers."

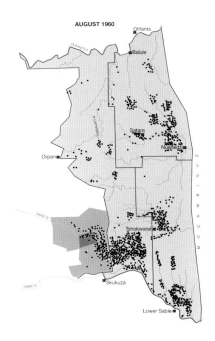

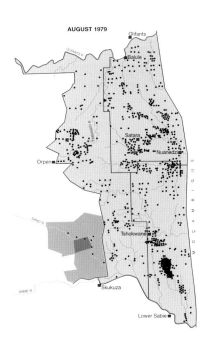

Two maps based on Ian Whyte's report illustrate the disappearance of the western wildebeest population of the Kruger Park: 1960, before the fence was closed and 1979, when only 752 wildebeest were counted. One dot represents 10 animals.

"Mr. Varty, perhaps you did not hear me," was the reply. "There the black people rule. Here the Nationalist Party rules." Checkmate!

The authorities simply did not understand that the habitat would not tolerate false divisions. John and Dave did not give up. Every year for the next ten years they persisted in making presentations to the various ministers of environmental affairs. However conservation and the environment remained a political bargaining chip and a weak portfolio. Fortunately there are signs that in the new South Africa conservation has been placed above politics. This is so necessary because water will always be in short supply on the southern tip of the African continent and will affect everyone, whatever race or colour, language or religion, human or animal.

Not until 1994 was the major fence between the Kruger Park and the private game reserves removed. But by then the animals that had survived the holocaust were conditioned to turning back at the fence. Early in 1996 however there was great excitement at Londolozi. Two breeding herds of elephants and two of buffalo had crossed the old fence line and for the first time in 36 years, Londolozi and the other Sabi Sand farms had a major influx of game from the KNP. The total number of elephants in the Sabi Sand had suddenly increased to over 200. James Marshall who had started working as a ranger at Londolozi in the early 80s and was visiting Londolozi as a consultant at the time believes that: "This could well be the start of a new pattern with more animals following the old seasonal migration routes." The question of whether the western population of wildebeest will ever recover to its former numbers remains unanswered.

In the late 70s John recognised that there was a fundamental problem with the farm Sparta. Using his business training, he sought the best advice he could find. And so they consulted the experts in the field. "Instinctively we felt we weren't getting the right answers," said Dave. "The scientists were looking in the wrong direction and thinking biologically instead of ecologically, studying segments of the problem and not the whole. They were looking at animal behaviour patterns, copulation, birth rates and so on. No one seemed to realise that in nature everything is inextricably linked."

John and Dave were two B.Com. graduates trained in business practices which made them question every explanation put forward. In fact their scientific ignorance gave them an edge over some of the scientists. They were not preconditioned in their thinking but, at the same time, they had acquired vast experience during their hunting days and remembered the many camp-fire discussions with their father. Dave comments: "What the scientists said didn't make sense.

"We searched for someone who could give us direction and then we heard about Dr. Ken Tinley. 'Don't go near him,' warned all the scientists. 'His theories are wild and unsubstantiated.' Of course we went. We found him in

Dr. Ken Tinley whose understanding of the ecology of Londolozi was to have such a profound effect. Following his advice, John and Dave turned the dried-out bushveld into a mosaic of grass and woodland. The result was a surge in bio-diversity and increase in the productivity of their farm. Ken's thesis on Gorongoza, written in the mid-70s is today being used for the restoration of Moçambique's great parks and reserves.

Left: A ground hornbill (*Bucorvus leadbeateri*) eyes strangers suspiciously.

Two spirally-coiled shells of giant land snails of the family Helicidae.

Above: The winged seeds of the large-fruited bushwillow *Combretum zeyheri*, the red bushwillow *Combretum apiculatum* and the wild teak/kiaat *Pterocarpus angolensis*.
Opposite from top left: *Dichrostachys cinerea* (sickle bush), *Adenium obesum* (impala lily), *Bauhinia galpinii* (pride-of-De Kaap), *Ochna natalitia* (rooihout), *Gardenia cornuta* (wild gardenia), *Acacia nilotica* (scented thorn), *Crinum delagoense* (Delagoa lily), *Ansellia africana* (leopard orchid), *Combretum microphyllum* (flame creeper).

Pretoria writing a thesis on Gorongoza, a game reserve in Moçambique. In him we found pure, distilled wisdom. He was an ecologist decades ahead of his time. A visionary genius. He took us from the dark days into the light. Meeting Ken was for both John and me perhaps one of the most enlightening moments of our lives. We shall remain forever grateful for his wisdom and ability to impart his knowledge to us."

Ken's skill was in his acute powers of observation and his ability to look at all segments of nature simultaneously. "He taught us about landscape patterns, geomorphology – how the land fitted together – about drainage lines and head-ward donga erosion which accelerated soil moisture loss," said Dave. "Then he went far and away beyond the thinking of the time. He believed in the mutual exchange of resources. He said: 'Survival of the reserves will depend on the attitudes of the people who live in adjacent areas, particularly as population pressures intensify. Don't think you can have a productive farm on one side of the fence and ignore people starving on the other side. It won't work.'"

Ken Tinley took Dave and John on a journey back to the time their grandfather had first visited Sparta. Their own farm together with the whole of the Sabi Sand is gentle rolling hill country through which winds 52 kilometres of the Sand river. Most of the tributaries as well as all the drainage lines at the base of the valleys are seasonal, flowing only for short periods after rain, although here and there, pools will last long into the dry season.

About 380 different tree species grow in the Sabi Sand, 200 of which reach tree height and the balance would be more typically described as shrubs. These include the wild date palm that grows close to the rivers and the lovely flowering aloes, impala lilies and the spectacular bauhinia, a scrambler which covers surrounding trees with brilliant orange flowers. The most common of all bush-veld trees are the acacias which are easily recognised by their small and sometimes tiny leaflets. In some species two or three thousand make up one compound leaf. Many acacias carry a multitude of different types of thorn and are covered in flowers ranging in colour from white to bright yellow in spring. There are 24 different species of acacia and nine different albizia which belong to the same family. Then there are 15 species of the easily recognised com-bretum with their four-winged seed pods which hang in clusters in colours ranging from brilliant red-brown to pale yellow and beige. Other common bushveld trees include the marula much loved by elephants, the slow-growing kiaat or wild teak, also appreciated by elephants and kudu, the lovely wild sycamore fig trees which grow on the banks of the Sand river and a profusion of shiny-leafed matumi or Transvaal teak trees right at the river's edge. Most striking of all are the towering jackalberry trees, often supporting a leopard orchid *Ansellia gigantea*, which greet Londolozi guests at all three camps along the Sand river.

The early spring leaves of the silver cluster-leaf *Terminalia sericea* and below, the blossom of *Acacia nilotica*.

Opposite: Top, a diagram illustrating the change in the vegetation from the sandy hilltops to the grassy seeplines and bottomlands at Londolozi. Below, buffalo graze on the seeplines which carry 70 percent of all Londolozi's wildlife during the winter months.

The aerial photographs of Sparta taken in the 1940s showed a wonderful mosaic of open grass-covered seeplines, or dambo systems, which divided the sandy crowns of mixed combretum and silver cluster-leaf terminalia from a narrow band of mature riverine forest. This habitat diversity maximised the productivity of the land. Sable, tsessebe, waterbuck, zebra, wildebeest, buffalo and ostrich favour the open grasslands. Giraffe, impala, nyala and kudu favour the woodlands.

In superimposing photographs taken in the late 70s on those taken 30 years earlier, the landscape is hardly recognisable. Over a period of 40 years the dongas had advanced up to 400 metres into the hillsides and the mosaic of grasslands and woodlands was replaced with choked thornveld. The acacia together with some of the broad-leafed trees and terminalia, which usually mark the upper edge of the seepline like a line of streetlights, had almost totally invaded the low-lying grasslands. The invasive small-leafed acacia, which with their long taproots could reach deep down into the earth to find water, were most responsible for this encroachment. The problem was that as this type of bush increased, it drew further on the water-table which dropped lower and lower. A drying-out ecosystem was the result.

"Ken spent several hours studying the aerial photographs with the aid of a stereoscope, which would have given him a three-dimensional illusion," remembers Dave. "He then selected various points and together we checked them out on the ground. Ken explained to us why our farm had become unproductive. He told us why our cheetah had run away. Why we were unlikely to keep sable. Why it would get worse and worse if our land was not properly managed. Then he directed us towards practical solutions, taking us to the head of an eroded ravine. 'This is where your problem started,' he told us. 'The donga is like a bath with the plug taken out. All the water is running out of this drain. You have to put the plug back in, repair the advancing headward erosion and restore the moisture in the soil if you are going to recover your grasslands.'

"Then Ken pointed to the line of terminalia. 'From below that line you have to take out all but a few of the acacias. Those that you leave behind will flourish, those that you pull out use to block your dongas, crowns facing up the slope. Water will percolate through the trees which will hold back the topsoil until the erosion is repaired. Then the grass will return.'

"He analysed the effect of erosion accelerated by cattle and wildlife tracks and by man. He showed us the difference in soil compositions in this gently undulating country which varied from red sandy hilltops to heavy black clays in the bottomlands. This mixture of soil types resulted in the rainwater from the hilltops quickly permeating through the sand until it reached the heavy black clay soils which act like a dam wall. The result was a seepline or, in times of heavy rain, a spongy vlei in which grasses flourished.

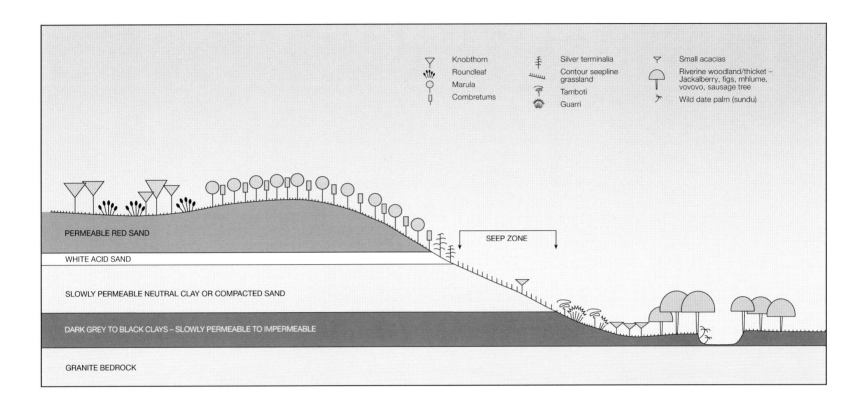

Knobthorn
Roundleaf
Marula
Combretums

Silver terminalia
Contour seepline grassland
Tamboti
Guarri

Small acacias
Riverine woodland/thicket –
Jackalberry, figs, mhlume, vovovo, sausage tree
Wild date palm (sundu)

SEEP ZONE

PERMEABLE RED SAND

WHITE ACID SAND

SLOWLY PERMEABLE NEUTRAL CLAY OR COMPACTED SAND

DARK GREY TO BLACK CLAYS – SLOWLY PERMEABLE TO IMPERMEABLE

GRANITE BEDROCK

"Ken explained how the initial damage had been done," said Dave. "Our grandparents had always travelled in July – the dry season. Not unnaturally, in their ox-wagons, the buckboard and later in their cars, they selected a route through open grasslands, on the seepline which would have been dry in winter. Exactly in the same areas where cattle had grazed and where the zebra and wildebeest had concentrated during their winter migration."

This over-utilization of the grasslands would have compacted the soils forming a secondary, artificial barrier and leading to increased run-off and the formation of eroded ravines or dongas. The grasslands below a compacted area, starved of access to moisture, would slowly dry out and would be ripe for scrub encroachment. This drying out process would also have been exacerbated by the long sequences of drought. "The concentration of game after the fence was put up accelerated the damage to the land," John added. "Although it was not long before the combination of these factors resulted in a major diminution of most species and the complete disappearance of others."

"Ken told us that everything we did should be aimed at increasing soil moisture," recalls Dave. "We would have to clear the acacia scrub, fill the dongas to prevent run-off, move our roads from seepline locations to sandy hilltops and close straight-line firebreaks down which water ran freely. Where we could not prevent run-off we would have to build dams. In later years when the river weakened as a result of the huge demands made on it upstream, we installed pumps to capture some of the high-flow water during floods and store it in our dams. The water pumped from the river would help safeguard hippo and riverine habitat through the next dry season. It would also percolate slowly back into the river, helping to maintain a high water-table on our lands and food for our animals in the winter.

"The seeplines are incredibly productive. During the winter months 70 percent of all our game is carried on those grass-covered bottomlands. Small wonder that when the grasses disappeared under the total invasion of acacias, the antelope and the predators also disappeared.

"From that one day with Tinley we understood that we would have to manage our seeplines and a large portion of the money we made from tourism would have to go back into restoring and rebuilding the habitat. This would entail a vast amount of work. The acacias weren't going to disappear and pulling them out and repairing the erosion would cost more than we cared to imagine." Initially they came in for severe criticism on many fronts but John and Dave were so convinced by Tinley's logic that they took up the challenge and immediately started implementing his plan.

John devoted himself to the task of land rehabilitation while Dave and Shan looked after the lodges and the visitors. "For every R1 we earned in tourism, we spent R1.20 on the land and we lived in overdraft," recalls Dave.

"John was always pushing to spend more money on the land while I was concerned about our bank balance. 'That doesn't matter,' was John's comment. 'It's irrelevant!' My query was 'How do we pay the bills?' John's reply was, 'We will, but first we'll fix the land.' It was an endless tug-of-war."

Land management entailed recording habitat and game population dynamics, the reintroduction of some species and the culling of others, maintaining daily records of rainfall and temperature, waterflows in the rivers and dam levels, and a dynamic and holistic approach to care of the land. It also meant employing a full-time game manager and a large workforce. "We had to keep one eye on the water-table and the other on the condition of our wildlife," said John.

"We went beyond ourselves for two decades," Dave commented. "I believe that is why Londolozi is such an unbelievable paradise of birds and animals today. We discovered that if you work with nature, her bounty is never ending. Conversely we had found that if you abuse nature, she will not forgive readily." Fortunately Dave and John had found Ken Tinley in time to reverse the damage. A new era had begun. This was the start of the model for conservation development. Coincidentally, the first sightings of the mother leopard began with the clearing programme. This leopard was to become legendary and was a prime example of the bounty of nature.

"Initially we thought that elephant relocation would assist in clearing some of the heavy bush and the thirsty trees which we had to remove before we could reclaim the grasslands," said Dave. "But very soon we discovered that 18 elephants in 57 000 hectares is asking too much – even of elephants!

"So we employed more and more people and used a bulldozer to remove the scrub, to fill dongas and to break up compacted ground. The bulldozer was also used to make shallow depressions where Ken showed us, with the aid of aerial maps, there once had been seeps or vleis. The results were immediate. Within six weeks the water-table rose. We were encouraged. We knew we were on the right track." It was not long before the old vleis filled and John and Dave could show others in the Sabi Sand what practical observation and gentle management of the habitat, working with nature, could produce.

The degradation of the habitat on Sparta was not isolated. Many areas of the bushveld had undergone enormous change as the acacia bush had slowly but relentlessly invaded the grasslands affected by man, his cattle and his fences. The Varty brothers, rebels against conventional thinking, had struck out on their own questioning why these changes to the habitat had taken place and then had endeavoured to repair their land. John and Dave, only just out of their teens, were wild, bursting with life and fun and always ready to party until dawn. Yet from an early age they had shown both an extraordinary sensitivity and serious side to their natures. They did not care about their worn and torn

Above: Crowned eagle, *Stephanoaetus coronatus*; and hoopoe, *Upupa epops*.

Opposite: Saddlebilled stork, *Ephippiorhynchus senegalensis*; little bee-eater, *Merops pusillus*; and wattled plover, *Vanellus senegallus*.

A feather from a guineafowl, *Numida meleagris*.

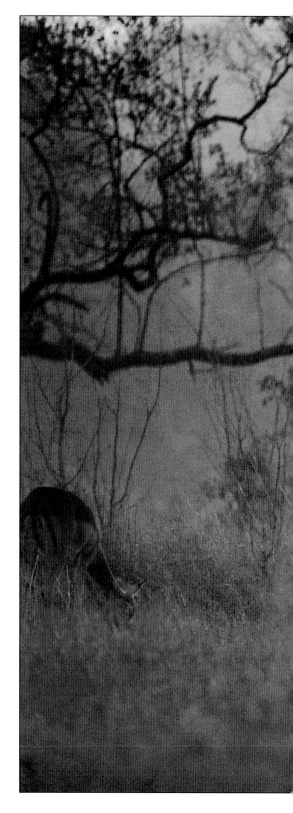

khaki clothes, they ate what came to hand and slept wherever there was a spare bed. But they cared deeply about the land and the wildlife. It was not long before many people started to recognise the immense value of the break-through the Varty brothers, with the aid of Ken Tinley, had made and the significance of their conservation initiative.

In the mid-70s many people came to Londolozi as guests and not only returned again and again but also helped Dave and John with their conservation programme and the development of their camp. Dave will never forget the day when a brand-new, out-of-the-box, bulldozer arrived at Londolozi. "I thought I was dreaming. Later in the day we received a phone call from Ross Parry-Davies who had helped us in our early days." He had devised a plan with Brian Hackney, managing director of LTA Construction and Dr. Zach de Beer, chairman of LTA, to lend Londolozi the 'dozer. Ross had been enchanted with Dave and John's determination to put back into the wild what man had taken out and repair the habitat that man had destroyed. He decided to do all he could to help them. The D7 bulldozer was put on site, ostensibly to build a dam which would be called the LTA dam. Whenever the bulldozer was not being used to build the dam, Dave and John could use it for their bush-clearing operations. As Dave says: "We literally worked around the clock." After the dam was completed Ross arranged for a second bulldozer to be sent to Londolozi which the Varty boys would pay for on a *quid pro quo* basis in exchange for accommodation. Ross says one of the most exciting moments of any project he had ever been associated with was detecting the first sign of seep over the contact of the sandy and clay soils soon after bush clearing had started.

Ross helped them build their first swimming-pool and organised a filtration plant for their water supply. He designed Londolozi's waterborne sewage system and showed Dave and John how to assemble the piping and connect it up to the toilets, baths and showers (which Ross arranged for them to remove from a building in Johannesburg which was being demolished). Ross drew a plan and showed them how to cut and thread the piping and then his entire family spent a Christmas at Londolozi helping Dave and John fit out the bathrooms. Ross also collected broken tiles from a builder friend of his and these were laid painstakingly one by one to create a mosaic on the floors and walls of the new bathrooms. Another friend Ian Simms, chairman of BP, supplied free diesel to accelerate the bush-clearing programme, while Peter Campbell of Nampak and Ian Hepburn helped put the Londolozi story onto film. "This was the kind of fantastic support we got from our friends," Dave says.

Work was started on the major operation of realigning roads. In the process of doing this it was discovered that the engineer who planned the Selati railtrack through the Sabie Game Reserve in the 1890s had known more about ecology than most people did 100 years later. He had placed his track exactly

Above: *Cassionympha cassius*, rainforest brown, and *Melanitis leda helena*, twilight brown.

Opposite: May 1979. Without elephants to help create a dynamic and changing habitat, the only solution was to use bulldozers to eradicate the thirsty bush that had encroached onto the grasslands at Londolozi. Six weeks after John and Dave started work on bush clearing, they saw the first sign of seep and dried-out vleis started to fill.

Previous pages: Cheetah and impala, two animals which enjoy different habitats.

on the watershed where it would cause least damage to ecosystems – exactly as Ken Tinley would have proposed. In contrast straight-line firebreak systems and the block-burning programmes of the 60s and 70s caused soil moisture loss, accelerating erosion and damaging habitat. Unfortunately it takes a great deal of money to reverse the results of these practices and even more regrettably, in many areas these practices still continue.

With the return of the game to the Londolozi grasslands, predators followed in abundance. Londolozi was back in the business of being able to show visitors a wonderful wildlife diversity. Once again there were lion, cheetah, hyena and wild dogs. Leopards began to be seen so regularly that these beautiful animals became the prime focus of all marketing operations. It was not long before the leopards of Londolozi became legendary worldwide.

Ken Tinley believed absolutely in the multiple use of resources and that the economic management of wilderness areas would create enormous opportunity for local communities. To quote from his report: "What is a problem in one sense is an opportunity in disguise. The dense knobthorn invasion of turf pastures in the Sabi Sand is a case in point. Their removal is required to restore pasture lands. But at the same time they are in demand as valuable timber and construction material by the neighbouring rural people. Many of the veld resources fall into this category including knobthorn and terminalia for poles, round-leaf kiaat root bases for carving, reeds and grasses for thatching, palm leaves for weaving, kiaat logs for furniture, firewood from clearing operations, medicinal plants, honey and meat and skins from culling."

Ken had warned them that on the scale they were working, an over-managed property could cause as much damage to the land as had mis-management. A balance had to be maintained and that involved a continuous juggling act which would involve culling. The sensible approach would be to provide meat for the local communities who also suffered from drought cycles. This was not, and is still not, allowed by the veterinary authorities because of foot-and-mouth disease. In the terrible drought of 1983, when the Sabi Sand was forced to reduce populations of impala and buffalo swiftly, a way round this regulation was found. Dried and cooked meat was allowed to leave the area – so a temporary field kitchen was constructed and altogether some 10 000 kilograms of cooked meat was sold cheaply to the surrounding communities. This action created extraordinary goodwill and interestingly, poaching was almost non-existent during the period. In a way this was not surprising. The tribal hunter had been motivated by the desire for food, clothing and shelter and had passed down his knowledge of animals and their habitats from generation to generation. He had to hunt in order to survive. What the Varty's were doing was reconnecting the communities with the wildlife utilisation circuit – a practice they were well schooled in.

Ken Tinley saw the tourism industry as a marvellous opportunity to retain the wilderness and its biodiversity while employing people in sustainable operations. He encouraged Dave and John to initiate opportunities where local people could be employed, and also where those with entrepreneurial flair could be helped to establish their own businesses. Today many people from local communities participate in Londolozi's ecotourism operation – in activities ranging from small businesses supplying Londolozi with products and services, to the employment of rangers and trackers, cameramen, line managers, teachers and nurses, chefs, mechanics, waiters and cleaners.

Thatching is just one of many examples of a sustainable small business operation supported by Londolozi. The thatched roofs at Londolozi, frequently damaged by weather and baboons, keep many people employed. Kefas Ndluli, a carpenter living not far away, collects wood from the Londolozi bush-clearing operations and employs ten Shangaan workmen in making furniture. Others run taxi services, transport businesses and vehicle maintenance workshops, while many women have learned to sew staff uniforms, make curtains and embroider bedspreads which Londolozi buys. Others weave and carve curios which are sold at the camps. Those with a feel for the soil have developed market gardens and supply Londolozi with fresh produce. One of Londolozi's chefs, Elmon Ndume, grows vegetables which he sells to Londolozi. John says: "When you get spinach for breakfast, lunch and dinner you know that Ndume is heavily invested in the spinach business!"

In the meantime John was still not satisfied. He compared wildlife on Londolozi with the game he had seen in Kenya and he wanted Londolozi to be the best. It was the same in their sporting careers. They were competitive. They wanted herds of elephants and wildebeest. Not just a few. Tinley was the first person they met who thought holistically. "Then I found David Hopcroft on a ranch in Kenya," said John. "He explained to me why our narrow seeplines did not attract wildebeest, which are sight animals and need to be able to watch for predators. They need high ground clear of bush to retreat to at night." The solution was to bulldoze more bush and link the seeplines together, or as in Kenya, they would need more elephants to clear the bush.

John learnt much more about elephants in Kenya where, he says, they have played a major role in habitat cycles. "Elephants are agents of change, converting woodlands to grasslands and then helping to distribute seeds and fertilise the regrowth of the forests. This has been happening over hundreds, perhaps thousands of years. It is estimated that Africa once supported 18 million elephants. Because man is a short-term species he has never had the opportunity to observe and understand these cycles. Elephant populations fluctuate naturally in balance with an ever-changing habitat. One of these cycles has been recorded in the Tsavo park in Kenya where the elephant population went up

Above and below: Ken Tinley's multi-utilisation of the wilderness philosophy provided jobs for many people. Game viewing was only a small part of his programme which included collecting firewood, honey and herbs, utilizing wood for carving and meat and skins from culling.

Opposite: Leopard, lion and hyena. All three predators provide great photographic opportunities at Londolozi.

and then crashed in the late 70s. The elephants cleared the bush in Tsavo. Because we only had 15 elephants in the Sabi Sand, we had to shake the habitat with bulldozers. But the effect was the same: a spectacular, and productive habitat. Just as change is the driving force of life, so too is change the catalyst to the productivity of a natural habitat. To hold elephant populations at a constant level is to lose out on the critical part that elephants play in maintaining a vibrant and dynamic habitat."

In 1977, just as Londolozi was turning the corner in its rehabilitation programme, Shan decided to take a year off to see something of the outside world. From the age of 15 she had been caught up totally with helping Dave and John in almost every aspect of their operation. Catering for up to 250 people in the bush, managing the camps, fund raising, planning projects, designing the lodges and the interior decor, opening their first shop, promoting Londolozi and processing the bookings. Now she set off to explore the world for a year. Eventually after nine months Dave was able to hitch a lift to London with one of his guests and bring Shan home. Two years later, and 10 years after that eventful meeting on the beach, Dave and Shan were married. On the eve of their wedding Dave wrote Shan a letter. Although it was only August 1980, and a long way to the Conservation Corporation days, Dave was already looking ahead to new challenges. He saw 'Londolozi as an achievement past us' and that they could 'accomplish wider things with our lives together'. He was 'a believer in achieving, creating, building up, and if necessary taking the knocks'. Most significant of all to Shan was his heartfelt desire to see her continue as an independent personality. "My dream had started when I was 15," said Shan. "My heart went out to a 17-year-old who I first saw looking over the ocean, still mourning the death of his father. It was from there that a friendship was built that grew into an all consuming passion and love for Dave and his vision for a small piece of land called Sparta."

Opposite: An old marula tree, its bark well polished by passing animals, ranks high in the diet of elephants which consume about 250 kilograms of vegetation a day. The elephants, which have browsed on its leaves and fruit, will process the seeds in their stomachs and will leave them to complete the germination process in their dung.

The early spring shoots of a marula tree, *Sclerocarya birrea*.

CLOSE ENCOUNTERS

The soul is the same in all living creatures
although the body of each is different.
— *Hippocrates.*

F THERE IS A SECOND reason why Londolozi developed into a wildlife paradise, it is the people. John and Dave showed a dedication and passion for the wild that was something out of Hemingway and inspired many young men and women whose love of the wild created a brilliant fund of wildlife experiences. The Vartys had no money and could not pay fancy salaries – in fact, hardly anything at all. But some remarkable young people were drawn to Londolozi and they were in their element in that fabulous bush country. Every moment they had to spare was spent learning, tracking, discovering – and everything they did, they did with enthusiasm and for the sheer love of it all.

The Londolozi standards were set by a group of rangers among whom were Ian Thomas, Peter Arnot, Warren Samuels, Map Ives, Ken Maggs, Mike Myers, Lex Hes, Waynne McLintock, Chris Badger, Paddy Hagelthorn and Ronnie McKelvey. Then there were men like Two-tone Sithole, Keys Mathebula, Richard Siwela, Kimbian Mnisi, Elmon Mhlongo, Julius Ngwenya and Sandros Sihlangu who started as trackers and developed into outstanding wildlife rangers. Some have moved away from Londolozi but all have retained their love of wildlife. "Londolozi has not lost out," says Shan. "They made a great contribution to building Londolozi and the legacy they left and the true stories of their adventures are part of the Londolozi tradition."

One of the great stories started with a leopard who would allow the rangers to follow her. Peter Arnot remembers the excitement when they first saw the mother leopard. "Mike Penman and I were following elephants down the Mshabene when a leopard cub came out of the bush, walked under Mike Penman's Land Rover and went to sleep. He couldn't move. The mother was in the long grass. We couldn't see her but we could hear her growling. I was also stuck because of the elephants behind us. Eventually the elephants moved off and we persuaded the cub to get out from under the Land Rover. When we went back she was still there. She was just a relaxed leopard who unwittingly started a dynasty that has given, and is still giving, incredible leopard viewing."

Until that time, rangers and visitors alike considered themselves lucky to catch a glimpse of a leopard in the thick riverine forests. Shan had seen leopard only twice in her first nine years at Londolozi. That changed with the appearance of the female leopard who became increasingly tolerant of the presence of the rangers and trackers. She began to permit humans into her secret world and would scratch herself up against the side of the Land Rover. Peter Arnot remembers how he would watch her tail pass within inches of his face. She would even use the vehicle as cover when hunting. One evening they found a large and very shy male with her. A few days later they were found mating and the following January two beautiful little cubs appeared.

Keys Mathebula (top) and Two-tone Sithole (above) were hunter naturalists of a bygone era. They had an intuitive understanding of wildlife and worked at Sparta for Boyd Varty during the wild days of hunting before turning their considerable bushveld skills to supporting Londolozi's photographic safaris.

Above, leopard cubs at Londolozi and opposite, a leopard secures her kill in the fork of a tree, well out of reach of hyena. The increased contact with leopards caused Londolozi's leopards to become tolerant of humans who no longer represented danger. At the same time they remained free-ranging, self-sufficient and wild. If a lion or hyena came too close or another leopard invaded its territory, the behaviour of a leopard would be likely to change instantly. Two of the most fearsome scenes in JV's film *Running Wild* show lions attacking the mother leopard, following her to the utmost branches of a tree, and a territorial dispute between two female leopards.

John and Elmon spent five years following the mother leopard, collecting footage for many videos and films he has produced starting with *The Silent Hunter*. One year they led a totally nocturnal existence, going out at 3 o'clock in the afternoon and following her through the night. At that time she was still very elusive. "We would lose her in the thick bush," John remembers, "and then find her again. And there were times when she would be far from passive, specially if there was another female leopard in her territory or if lions were about. We put in incredible hours and she got used to vehicles and to us." Elmon and John, or JV as he has become known, have spent more time with leopards than any other human beings. The result is the spectacular footage that they have obtained of the mother leopard who brought nine sets of cubs into the world, of her grooming her cubs and teaching them to hunt, of her challenging another female leopard in a territorial dispute and of her eventually being attacked and mortally wounded by lions.

Paddy Hagelthorn remembers the evening when he and Elmon went off to track the leopard who they hadn't seen for a few days. They found the spoor which led them into very thick bush. "We had actually given up," said Paddy, "and were walking back to the Land Rover when suddenly something made us turn around. There, behind us was the leopard, tracking us! We went on walking and eventually came to a clearing near a pan. Both of us sat down, and so did the leopard, who proceeded to groom herself not three metres from us. We slipped out quietly and came back later with guests. She was still there, lazing and grooming herself. That was one of the most phenomenal experiences I ever had at Londolozi."

The story of the mother leopard was to make Londolozi internationally famous. A magazine article by Peter Johnson and Alf Wannenberg appeared in *Geo*, the world's foremost natural history magazine. After the article appeared, it was picked up by just about every wildlife magazine in the world, and must have been read by over 40 million people. The story was also documented by Lex Hes in his book *The Leopards of Londolozi* which covers the first three generations of the dynasty, and it was told on film and video.

Dave and John are well aware of the immense gift they received from nature. "It was the start of a remarkable relationship between humans and animals unprecedented in the wild. We built an industry around the legacy from the mother leopard. She gave birth to nine sets of cubs and a further twelve sets of cubs from her progeny have been recorded on Londolozi. One of our rangers has a full-time job tracking and recording leopard behaviour. People from all over the world come to see them. They are wild and free but they have learnt to tolerate humans and we are immensely richer for the joy they give us and our many visitors."

Londolozi's management ethic was not to give names to animals except,

Above: Bird eggs. Scimitarbilled wood-hoopoe, *Rhinopomastus cyanomelas*; redchested cuckoo or Piet-my-vrou, *Cuculus solitarius*, laid in the same nest with those of a whitethroated robin *Cossypha humeralis*; plumcoloured starling, *Cinnyricinclus leucogaster*; goldenbreasted bunting, *Emberiza flaviventris*; blackeyed bulbul, *Pycnonotus barbatus*. Eggs actual size.

People come from all over the world to see Londolozi's leopards and are never disappointed. The cats are incredibly beautiful and exciting, the cubs fun to watch. The leopard cub (right), found the bonnet of a Land Rover a convenient landing stage on its way down from a tree. Below: A single flower from a sjambok pod tree, *Cassia abbreviata*.

A flapnecked chameleon (left) with its prehensile tail – and a long flickering tongue ready to lash out at unsuspecting insects. It has been estimated that insects make up 70 percent of all animal life and while some people recoil with horror at the sight of a scorpion or a spider, a little curiosity will be well rewarded.

Feathers of a blackheaded oriole.

as indigenous people have done through time, according to some physical characteristic or a specific personality trait. Peter Arnot did, however, give names to a few animals he got to know well. "There was an elephant I called 458," he said. "He had been shot in the face – the bullet had ricocheted inside his skull, missed his eye and had come out through the top of his head. We patched him up – after darting him." Then there was Elvis who was simply the biggest lion on record. "When I first saw him he was lying across the road with his nose in the grass on one side and his tail in the grass on the other side. He was superb. Never a hair out of place, not a scratch or a broken tooth. Even his nails looked manicured! It's the only time I've ever seen females kowtow – but they did to him. There was not a male in the entire Sabi Sand who did not go in fear of Elvis. If they did cross his path they got so beaten up they looked like George Foreman for months!"

Most exciting of all was a black-maned lion who came in from the Kruger Park in his prime. Most lions form a coalition with one or two others to hold a territory. Big Black, as he was described by the rangers, was different. Single-handed, he dominated the Londolozi lands for three years and established a strong genetic strain of black-maned lions. "He wasn't a particularly big lion but he was value for money," recalls Peter. "I would have liked to have put him on our staff. People came to Londolozi just to be charged by Big Black. I was never sure whether he was just an enthusiastic amateur or a vegetarian but he never ate anyone although he would invariably charge our vehicles. It's no joke having a lion coming at you full blast. It tends to focus your attention! We didn't bother with rifles when we went looking for Big Black. We took sawn-off shotguns."

Lex Hes had been away on Marion Island for nine months and on his return he discounted the stories of Big Black. He thought they were all exaggerations. Then he took out a party of newly-arrived guests from Germany. Elmon was with him and the first thing that happened was they were charged by an elephant. Then they picked up the spoor of lion. "Elmon and I got out of the Land Rover to track the lions," Lex told us. "It was open country and our guests could see us clearly. Elmon warned me that he had recognised Big Black's spoor, but I was still confident that the lion would back off if we found him. We had walked about 100 metres when Big Black suddenly came out from behind a bush and charged. Everyone could see us. We stood our ground and the lion stopped just a metre away. Eye to eye. Almost nose to nose. We were in a deadly battle of wills. Just then we heard a shout from the Land Rover behind us. 'Ve've had enough. Zat vill do. Ve vant to go home now!' One of the guests was standing up waving her hands to get our attention. Fortunately Ian Thomas drove up then and helped us out of the tight spot we were in. To this day I don't know whether she realised we were facing death or if she thought it was a staged performance!"

Peter Arnot, a ranger at Londolozi in the 80s says of the big black-maned lion who ruled Londolozi for nearly three years: "Big Black made more men out of boys, myself included, than the South African army ever did – or Cindy Crawford for that matter!"

Opposite: Elvis. Exciting. Fearsome. But also magnificent.

Above: A puff-adder, definitely not to be handled except by an expert. Wild dog are usually only found in family groups or hunting packs.

Opposite: For the most part nature should be left to its own devices. Occasionally, however, the call to intervene is too strong to ignore. Top, Londolozi rangers assist a bedraggled giraffe which had slipped on the wet rocks when crossing the Sand river. Centre, a ranger cleans the wound after vet Roy Bengis had removed a snare of steel cable that had cut deep into the leg of a bull rhino. Bottom, Lex Hes assists in a research programme on Wahlberg's eagles.

One day Lex saw Big Black being chased across the Sand river by two younger males. He was no longer in his prime and was forced to give way to the next generation. A few weeks later he was killed on a neighbouring farm. "Four of our rangers resigned on the spot," remembers Dave. "They could not imagine game viewing without the incredible excitement that he provided. Back in Johannesburg, some of Londolozi's friends wept when they heard the news of the demise of this majestic beast."

Hugh Marshall, who had left the concrete jungle of Johannesburg and a career in insurance, had managed to get through the Londolozi ranger's examinations on the strength of his knowledge of birds. He remembers his most embarrassing moment in the bush. He had noticed from the noise of birds that there was a snake under a nearby bush. He had pointed out the puff-adder to his guests and spent quite a few minutes telling them just how dangerous and poisonous the snake was, when Paddy Hagelthorn drove up. Paddy was the next-best thing to a professional snake handler and he stepped out of his Land Rover, went into the bush and picked up the snake. He then proceeded to show the guests the puff-adder at close range. Hugh was struck dumb.

Paddy earned quite a reputation as a ranger. He told us that he was never quite sure whether he had the luck of the Irish or whether there were some psychic powers involved. "Not that I believe in them," says Paddy. But some of his sightings were almost too good to be true. "When I was a fairly new ranger I had a run of good game finding. So much so that the other rangers used to ask me what I would find next. On one occasion I said 'this afternoon we'll find cheetah and cubs'. And we did. Then I promised wild dog which we hadn't seen for 18 months and they were one of the first animals we found. Then I got really cocky and told Hugh Marshall that at 7.28 he would find elephants, which we hadn't seen for quite a while. The next morning he came onto the radio and said he had bumped into elephants. I looked at my watch. It was 7.28!"

Peter Arnot remembers that not all game drives are successful in terms of game viewing. "We never saw a single thing, not even a squirrel, on one of the best safaris we ever had. The guests were unimpressed, I was dispirited and the tracker felt he should resign. He just did not know what was happening – over three hours of nothing. It was a freak. And then, probably because I lost concentration, I drove the Land Rover into the deepest part of the river and we got stuck right up to the chassis. We couldn't move. I took the rifle and gave it to the guy who was doing most of the grumbling and told him to go 20 yards upstream and look out for crocs. Then I got the girls to hitch up their skirts and the guys were off with their shirts and we started digging. It took us two hours to get out. When we got back we were covered in mud but when I bought drinks there was not a grumble. They had had so much fun that the next party asked if they too could have the 'river' experience!" Dave and John learnt a very good lesson from the incident and that is to involve the guests in activities and encourage them to participate in locating animals, in finding their way when walking and in identifying species for themselves.

The life of a ranger wasn't just about taking care of visitors – it also involved the care of animals. It seems impossible that a five metre tall giraffe could drown in a river only a few centimetres deep but the flat rocks in the Sand river are notoriously slippery when wet and every now and then a giraffe slips when crossing the river. If it does not die by drowning, the extreme blood pressure that builds up when it is prostrate would soon lead to brain damage and death. On one occasion JV had a major task trying to help a giraffe that had slipped and fallen while crossing the river. JV knew the helpless animal did not have long to live. He radioed for a bulldozer to help move the 1000 kilogram animal and was able to push it to the river bank where it could help itself into an upright position. That giraffe made a full recovery but sometimes the rangers were too late to save animals in a similar predicament.

Once they found a badly injured rhinoceros that had been caught in a poacher's snare. The wire had cut deeply into its leg. After darting the suffering beast, veterinarian Roy Bengis quickly removed the wire and packed the wound with antibiotics. There was no chance of stitching the huge gash: no human hand could push a needle through its tough hide. An hour later, after the antidote was administered, the rhino struggled to its feet and joined its mate which had been waiting a little too closely for their comfort. The rhino, easily identified by the scar on its leg, made a full recovery.

Some of the rangers like Gary Lotter first visited Londolozi when they were youngsters. Gary graduated with a B.Sc. in botany and zoology and then decided to forsake an academic life in favour of Londolozi. Others, like Lex Hes, had no qualifications but with a tenacity and persistence that won Shan's heart, were given the opportunity. Lex learnt his bush lore in the field, studying every bird, insect, flower, tree and animal until he became an expert. Then there was Tony Adams who came to Londolozi with his wife Dee. Six months later Dee asked if she could be considered for a job as a ranger. With a university degree in biology and a sincere one-to-one ability to communicate, she sailed through the exams and became Londolozi's first woman ranger. To this day John says Dee is his best graduate in driving, bush knowledge and weapon handling.

In the early days, life was a real rough and tumble affair. The rangers lived in what is today the store-room. Peter Arnot will never forget the night Big Black visited the camp. "I met him outside my room and he growled at me. I nearly fainted! I got inside fast and he started roaring. The guy in the next room was convinced he was going to come straight through the thin pole and daub walls."

Lex remembers the snakes that would frequent their room, probably after the rats and mice. "There were plenty of bullet holes in the corrugated roof from

Top: The spotted hyena, heavily built and more than a match for leopard and the smaller carnivores, frequently steals a kill. It is an opportunist, an accomplished hunter and an adaptable scavenger. The clan has a well-organised and advanced social system led by the matriarch. The hyena's eerie whoops, yells and giggles are understandably often associated with witchcraft.

Above: A white rhino after a rainstorm at Londolozi.

Opposite: A leopard cub's inquisitive and fearless nature could lead it into trouble.

people trying to shoot snakes in the rafters." Those days were very special – guests were largely South Africans although even in those early days people came from all over the world. The camaraderie amongst the rangers and camp staff was tremendous. Many of the old staff have gone their different ways but one thing that hasn't changed is the spirit that exists amongst the staff at Londolozi and the bond between Londolozi and its many regular visitors.

The summer of 1996 was one of the most memorable seasons for the whole of South Africa. Once it started to rain it never stopped. Dams, even big ones, filled up within a few weeks and in the bushveld the rivers started to flow again and the water-table came up and up. By the end of summer the grass was not quite as tall as 'an elephant's eye', but it was lush and inviting.

Out on a walk with Shan and a few visitors after this wonderful rainy season, Dave described how the eroded ravines on Londolozi were successfully plugged in the late 70s. Previously there had been ugly gashes in the hillsides with rainwater not only draining quickly away but also taking topsoil with it. They had built mini-dams all the way down the valleys, slowing down the pace of the run-off. The result was that the riverine vegetation had regrown to the water's edge and once again the streams ran clear.

Shan gave an account of the morning's outing. "We had not walked more than half a kilometre on a grassy slope that was spongy and wet underfoot, when we saw a pair of hyena watching us. A little further on we found them following closely behind. They were stalking us. Then we saw a pair of rhinos grazing directly ahead. Just then a Land Rover came bouncing down the hill towards us. The ranger, Sandros, called out to Dave that there were two lions a few hundred metres to the left and on the top of the hill there were three leopards, a mother and two cubs. Deciding that discretion was the better part of valour, we hitched a lift back to our own vehicle. Once we had climbed aboard, we had a 'grandstand' view of the rhinos and the lions.

"We decided to give up walking and drive to the leopards. And there they were, the mother totally relaxed, stretched out on the trunk of a marula tree recently knocked down by elephants. The two cubs never kept still for a second: flying through the air to pounce on an unsuspecting butterfly, leaping to the highest branches which would collapse under their weight, tumbling and rolling in playful combat and returning to receive maternal approval. They were learning the skills of survival and enjoying every moment. We sat spellbound at the beauty and the sheer *joie de vivre.*"

Dave talked about nature's bounty. How rewarded they were at Londolozi where nature had not been abused. There had been many spin-offs starting from the time that they had repaired the dongas. The land had become so much more productive. "This morning's experience is a typical example of nature's virtuous cycle," said Dave. "When we patched the donga and stopped the run-

In the early 70s few elephants roamed Londolozi. Elephants which once travelled vast distances in the Kruger Park and sometimes ventured through the gorges into Moçambique, had been stopped from reaching the Sand river at the veterinary fence put up in the early 60s. Thirty years later, a combination of the removal of the western veterinary fence in 1994 and the cessation of culling in 1996 has resulted in excellent recolonisation of the Londolozi area where up to 200 elephants now roam freely. Cheetah, which prefer open grasslands to the thick bush that had invaded Londolozi, fled to the south in the 60s and early 70s but with the repair of the habitat, they have returned.

off we increased the effective rainfall. The result is the cover had improved and more buffalo and elephants had come in attracted by the long grass."

Nature's virtuous cycle doesn't end there. The predators benefit from the productivity of their prey. Visitors have the benefit of sitting or moving slowly and watching an abundance of wildlife instead of careering about searching for a few animals. Dave has seen the results of caring for the land. "We wouldn't be in the wonderful position we are in now, where we enjoy magnificent wildlife viewing including lion, leopard, elephant, rhino and buffalo, if it had not been for the groundwork we put in during the 70s."

Steve Sanders, a property developer from Naples, Florida, and his wife Jane Ellen, went on a fairly typical game drive at Londolozi. Back in his cottage he wrote up his diary: "People come to Africa and stay for weeks just to catch a glimpse of the Big Five: rhino, elephant, Cape buffalo, lion and leopard. We've already seen so much and it is only nine o'clock in the morning. Elmon took us out after an early five o'clock wake-up call followed by a quick tea on the verandah – a better game driver cannot be found in all of Africa. We had driven roughly six kilometres over rolling terrain covered with acacia before we discovered our first significant animals – four young bull elephants. We watched these massive creatures uproot trees and feed on shrubs and grass from distances of no more than 30 metres. We travelled another kilometre before we found a large white rhino. Elmon then took us to a spot where he had literally smelt a kill. The odour was rank when we found the lion on the zebra but he had picked up the smell some distance away and led us straight in. We tracked the lion after it had dragged the kill into the bush, until it was too thick for us to go any further. When the Land Rover stopped, we could hear what sounded like branches snapping in two. It turned out to be hyena breaking the bones of the zebra.

"Next we saw a truly remarkable sight: a pride of lions, consisting of a male, female and four cubs, was taking a nap in the sun in a dry riverbed. Above them was a female leopard, who was treed and apparently afraid to be on the ground with the lions so near. Finally she got up her courage and leapt from the tree and was off in a flash. The male lion, which had been oblivious to the sound of the Land Rover, immediately got to his feet at the sound made by the leopard. After a shake and a stretch he went back to sleep. Lastly Elmon showed us a mother cheetah and four cubs feeding on a small impala she had killed 15 minutes before we got there. Four cubs are rare for a cheetah but they were all healthy and maybe six to seven months old. We watched them feed and then headed in for breakfast ourselves. The only problem with a morning like today's is – what do they do for an encore?" (In fact on their next drive they found themselves surrounded by a herd of Cape buffalo.)

Barbara and Ken Godbert from Cumberland in England were thrilled with their first day at Londolozi. They watched a female leopard who permitted them

Seventy years ago the lion population in the area now known as the Sabi Sand was reported as having increased to 3000 – no doubt encouraged by the plentiful supply of food in the form of cattle. Commercial ranching stopped in 1938 after the foot-and-mouth disease outbreak. Then with the disappearance of wildebeest in the early 60s, the lions also disappeared. (Although Sparta was a hunting camp, in the 20 years between 1942 and 1962, Madeleine Varty's game book records only 15 lions shot.) With the start of photographic safaris, lions became more accustomed to humans and as a result were frequently seen.

to track her back to where her cubs were hidden amongst the rocks in a dry riverbed. Then she brought out her cubs and attended to their morning's grooming. Later in the day they came upon three lions which had just killed a porcupine. The little animal had defended itself with all its limited abilities; one lion had a major task removing the quills that had successfully hit their target.

You never know what you are going to see next when you are on a game drive. On one occasion with Elmon and JV, Steve Sanders stopped after no more than 50 yards – to watch a family of dwarf mongooses who were happily scampering about until they saw a martial eagle giving the inquisitive but shy little animals his full attention. As he flew off, a family of warthog took to their heels with their tails flying. The martial eagle would have been quite comfortable taking out a piglet rather than a mongoose!

A kilometre further on they came to a dam with a few crocodile and hippo. What caught their attention, however, was a colony of whitefronted bee-eaters. These brightly coloured little birds, painted in shades of green, blue, tan, white and red, had dug their metre-long burrows into a bank just below the dam wall. Now they were rushing to and fro catching insects and taking food to their nestlings safely ensconced in the river bank. Back on the road JV pointed out elephant droppings, amongst which were half a dozen wonderfully healthy marula seedlings. "So many people see elephants as destructive," JV told them. "But here is a perfect example of the elephant's ability to reconstruct the natural forest. They may knock down a marula tree and eat the fruit. But the seeds start the germination process in their stomachs and from one tree, a whole forest can be reborn."

While JV was talking they noticed a dark chanting goshawk in a tree above them. They passed by waterbuck, impala, wildebeest and zebra. JV said that every animal has a 'flight mechanism' so that the herd can follow its leader away from danger. Waterbuck have a distinctive white 'target' imprinted on their rear, impala and kudu have flashing white tails, warthogs hold their tails high. Zebra are a little different. When they flee from danger they keep close together and the mass of stripes tends to confuse the predator. Leopards, lions and servals have distinct black and white markings on the backs of their ears for the cubs to follow.

JV and his party crossed a dry riverbed and discovered a supremely indifferent and stunningly beautiful leopard. She had just set out on her evening's hunt. They followed the young leopard through thicker and thicker bush. The birds started to chatter. A whole tree of European swallows, gathering before their migration north, came to life. An owl hooted. And then the full moon came out from behind some clouds. An impala sounded the alarm nearby and the leopard ran off immediately to investigate. John explained that while she was still feeding her cubs she would not take any chances when hunting.

So little is known about inter-species communication but as our knowledge of sociobiology increases the evidence that it exists builds up. Recent field studies have shown that dwarf mongooses rely on an 'all clear' call from yellowbilled hornbill before venturing out of their burrows in the early morning. If a martial eagle should be around, yellowbilled hornbills will stay quiet and the little mongooses will stay safely underground.

Porcupine quills.

She would look for a young impala, a duiker or even a hare. She would take her kill up a tree, perhaps eat a little and then fetch her cubs. They listened to the fierynecked nightjar singing its plaintive song and then started back to camp. On the return journey they found thirteen lions just waking up for their nocturnal activities and right outside the camp an old dark giraffe had taken up his night's abode. Such is a normal day at Londolozi.

That evening around the camp fire John talked about leopards. The young mother they had seen that day was instinctively good at looking after her cubs. They would have a fair chance of surviving their first year. Another leopard had lost her two lovely little cubs when they were just a few weeks old. She had not hidden them well and before they were old enough to escape danger hyena had taken them.

Londolozi's game viewing and the interpretive skills of the rangers combine to make an extraordinary wildlife experience. "There's nothing to touch the challenge of the search in that lovely wilderness and the excitement of discovery," says Dave. "You may see millions of wildebeest and zebra in the Masai Mara and the Serengeti, thousands of elephants at Chobe, hundreds of buffalo in the Luangwa valley. But right here there's something different around every corner. It's the unexpected, the closeness and the sheer magic of the biodiversity that's so fascinating."

Opposite: Juvenile scrub hares are vulnerable to leopard and smaller carnivores.

Opposite below: A fierynecked nightjar and a giraffe silhouetted against the sunset.

Cape white-eye nest, *Zosterops pallidus*.

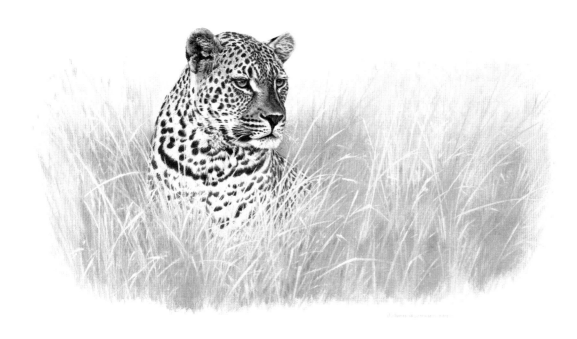

LIFE AT LONDOLOZI

The life so short, the craft so long to learn.
— *Hippocrates*

HERE IS BUT ONE WAY to survive a bushveld existence and that is to tune into nature and take things that happen in your stride," says Shan. "Many incidents weren't funny at all. Some were exciting, some frightening. But afterwards there were two things you could do. Forget about what had happened or laugh. Mostly people laughed, just occasionally there were events that affected people so deeply they preferred to forget."

Shan says of her early bushveld days: "The communal prefab we all shared until after we married was a great nursery school in which to learn how to cope with Africa." Ablutions consisted of a shower rose under a large tree and an occasional bath in a galvanised tub for which they would draw straws. The toilet, which at one time lost its seat to the ubiquitous appetite of a hyena, was open to the stars, while Shan's only mirror hung from a branch in that great outdoor bathroom. One winter in the 70s, it was so cold that John decided to make bricks and insulate the prefab against the weather. At first it worked well, but then the rats found the space between the prefab wall and the newly laid bricks. After the rats came the snakes. "We would have gang wars going on right next to our pillows," laughs Shan.

"At the start we were a group of like-minded youngsters with an average age of 24. The combination of youth, naivety, ignorance and an abundance of enthusiasm and energy could have spelt disaster. We made mistakes. But we learnt fast. There was only one work ethic: if you could dream it, you could do it. The result was we often took on challenges a few sizes too big for us. But things got done."

Against all odds the Vartys managed to get the business going. Today if you put the same set of parameters in front of any entrepreneur he would consider the task of establishing an upmarket game lodge for 48 guests and 150 staff impossible. They had no capital for development. The farm Sparta was a severely downgraded asset badly in need of funds to restore the habitat and the wildlife was poor. On one occasion in those early years they heard the roar of lions near the camp some time after midnight. Lions had taken down a buffalo. It was too good an opportunity to miss so they woke their guests, bundled them into a Land Rover and took them game viewing in their pyjamas. What they didn't anticipate was that the battery of the Land Rover would go flat and they would have to sit it out in the cold until dawn!

With the help of Ken Tinley, John and Dave had turned around the Londolozi game reserve. Game viewing was superb. "We had all the Big Five and just about all the species of antelope that had previously inhabited the bushveld east of the Drakensberg," said Dave. It was time to focus on the hospitality side of the business and a small group of girls took on this task.

Above: The early days at Londolozi. Summer or winter their 'bathroom' was a shower hooked into a tree. Shan Watson with a baby impala. Opposite: A redbilled oxpecker, *Promerops cafer*, investigates the skin of a rhinoceros for parasites.

Carissa bispinosa, forest num-num.

Top: Wonderful evenings were had around the boma fire. Standing, André Goosen and Lex Hes, seated Mike Myers playing the guitar, Janine Ovendale, Shan, Ve Mascall and John, and in front, Dave.

Above: Ian Thomas and his son Clyde who was born at Londolozi. Ian became one of the legends of Londolozi with his wonderful camp-fire stories, specially about Big Black, which he subsequently used, when he developed a series of lectures which compared lion behaviour in the wilderness with life in the boardroom.

A warthog tusk.

"In the 70s when it came to designing, building and decorating we did it all," Shan says. "There were no funds to bring in specialists. We drew our plans in the sand, made the bricks, laid them, plastered and painted. Nobody had one single task." Shan and Ve Mascall, JV's lovely girlfriend, later joined by Janine Ovendale, set the pace. They did the catering and reception and started the shop with painted St. Augustine wine boxes as shelving. They also looked after both guests and staff. "We gave classes to the children during the day and taught literacy to our staff at night. We learnt to help with health problems, treating anything from malaria, snake bites, a fishhook through a finger, syphilis, or bringing babies into the world. We acted as marriage guidance counsellors and there were occasions when we helped people overcome emotional problems – not only the lovelorn rangers. Possibly because Londolozi was seen by some as a means of escape from the trials and tribulations of life, there were also suicides. Moira Thomas, who worked with us for eight years, was invaluable with her skills as a qualified nursing sister."

"In a few months we had three extraordinary incidents," says Dave. "Shan was always in the thick of things, always totally unflappable and able to help people and think and act decisively. We had a lightning strike on the deck of Main Camp when 40 people were having tea. The strike set the thatched roof on fire. We grabbed fire extinguishers, put out the fire, tended the injured, served the tea, cut the cake – all with a façade of calm which Shan did extraordinarily well. The Londolozi philosophy is the show must go on.

"Not long after that an aircraft lost an engine on take-off. Shan was first at the airstrip rescuing the shocked passengers. Fortunately all eight walked away from the crash unscathed. Then we had a buffalo in camp. On return from a game drive Pat Hinde and his wife May walked straight into it. The buffalo charged May; one horn goring her right thigh and Pat without any thought for his own life leapt onto the animal's back, grabbed his horns and hung on for all he was worth. Pat thought he had no chance of surviving as the huge animal tried to rid himself of his unwanted passenger. In the melee of human and animal bodies, Warren Samuels, their ranger, killed the buffalo stone dead with a brilliant shot at point blank range. Pat Hinde, chairman of a leading motor dealer, presented Warren with a brand new Toyota as a reward, not only for saving their lives but for curing him of a rare and extremely painful form of rheumatism. The adrenaline that pumped through his body in those frightening few moments put the disease into remission and 12 years later it has not returned. Today it would be extremely difficult for a wild animal to get past the guards who unfailingly escort visitors to their chalets," says Dave, "but the camps are open and after dark guests should never move about without a guard."

There was a need to improve catering from the early 'cans and impala' standards. Lynn Melle arrived with a university degree in home economics, daunting Shan whose early interests had been speech and drama and not the kitchen. The lovely and vibrant Lynn caused quite a stir amongst the rangers who jostled for position to win her attentions. Lex Hes who, for the first nine months he was at Londolozi, had been too shy to open his mouth, was captivated. It was not long before he came out a clear winner and married Lynn.

Over the next decade a group of talented women gave their time, energy and skills to Londolozi. They were caring and beautiful, zany and clearheaded, practical and emotional. They knew how to deal with the hunky, high-powered rangers, how to cope in emergencies and how to live life to the full.

After Dave and Shan were married in 1980, they planned their own house on the Sand river. Top priority for Shan was that every bedroom should have its own bathroom. There would be no more sharing of the bathtub. As with all other construction at Londolozi, their house was built on a shoestring. But everyone helped. Plans were once again drawn in the sand, they made the bricks and got going. Despite these disadvantages, having their own home was a wonderful luxury although their gruelling schedule seldom changed; up usually at dawn, sometimes even earlier, a long day and late to bed. One morning when they had a day off, Shan remarked to Dave how beautiful it was waking to the sounds of birds. He quickly disillusioned her. They were alarm calls warning that a black mamba was in the garden.

Snakes were always a problem – particularly after Bronwyn was born in 1983 and Boyd two years later. The children needed to be carefully watched over. At Londolozi there was a wonderful support network led by Lucy, their Shangaan nanny. The children were never left alone for a second. Once when jogging through one of the dry riverbeds Shan found herself looking straight into the throat of a mamba. She has never run so fast in her life!

A few years later Dave and Boyd had a narrow shave with a reptile. It had been agreed between Dave and his children that despite the end of the hunting era, he should pass on the skills of the hunt just as he had been taught when he was young. There were so many valuable lessons to be learnt, none of which would be found in text books. They would hunt only impala which, because of their numbers, were being harvested on a regular basis in the Sabi Sand. One morning when Dave and Boyd went out they found an ideal situation for closing in on a herd of impala. They were downwind and would be well hidden by a termite mound. Boyd, kneeling on the mound, took aim and fired. One impala dropped. The rest fled. The next second Dave heard his son say: "Oh! Shit dad! Snake!" Dave, kneeling right behind his son was looking over Boyd's head and it took a second or two before he was able to locate the deadly black mamba over two metres in length and as fat as a man's wrist. It was between them and in the process of slowly coiling itself around Boyd's legs. Young as he was Boyd knew that his only chance was to stay dead still. The mamba could

After Shan and Dave moved into their house, there was another invasion. "It was a very dry season and we had an influx of rats," says Shan. "They ate everything; our tupperware, our lovely antique yellow-wood, the carpet, bath soap, even corks. They ate holes in our doors. After the rats came the owls, the snakes – and scorpions. We had our own in-house ecosystem."

Protogoniomorpha parhassus, common mother-of-pearl.

Above: A bateleur, *Terathopius ecaudatus,* the juggler of the sky, includes reptiles of all varieties in its diet.

Opposite: Snakes at Londolozi, some gentle and inoffensive, others aggressive when disturbed. From top left to bottom right: a vine snake, black mamba, variegated bush snake, tiger snake, striped skaapsteker snake, snouted night adder.

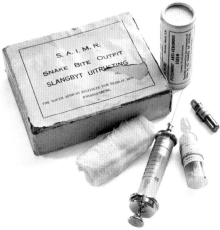

The treatment for snake bite has hardly changed over the years.

have risen up about two-thirds of its length and a strike, particularly on the upper body, would have been lethal. In an extraordinary display of self-control, neither moved a muscle as Dave watched in horror. He was utterly helpless. For both of them it felt like a lifetime. But sensing no threat, the mamba relaxed, unwound itself from Boyd's legs and continued on its way. Once it was out of striking range Dave told Boyd to run. He still does not know how the gun got from his 11-year-old son's hand into his.

In the dry season elephants often visited the camps. Boyd and Bronwyn were with their teacher, Rose Parsons, taking a swim in the pool at John's house when elephants came trumpeting up for a drink. "We got out fast," says Rose. But the pool was not built for elephants and when they left it was badly cracked with the water draining out. The swimming-pool was not the only casualty from the gentle intentions of a heavy-weight pachyderm.

When Bronwyn and Boyd started school in Johannesburg Shan found the journeys back and forth, often at the end of long weekends, time-consuming and often dangerous. She decided that the solution was to learn to fly. One evening she told Dave and John of her intentions. "As usual," says Shan, "John's retort was quick." "With due respect, Shanny," he said, "if you had wanted to fly you should have done it ages ago. You're much too old." Shan was 28 and confident of her ability. She went ahead and got her licence. It was not long before a single-engined Cessna 182 was parked on the Londolozi airstrip. "One morning," remembers Shan, "we went up to the airstrip to see our lovely little aircraft about a hundred metres from its usual mooring position. I asked Dave why he had moved it which of course he denied. On closer inspection we discovered the mangled remains of the aircraft which an elephant had decided was about his fighting weight."

In fact John was doing no more than instinctively trying to protect Shan from the dangers of flying. He has the highest regard for her abilities. "Shan fits into any situation with any people and once she takes on a task she follows it through to the end. I remember once asking Shan to sew Ben Abruzzo's hot-air balloon together after it had ripped to pieces on the sharp hard thorns of *Acacia nilotica* when they landed in a forest of these trees. Shan sewed miles and miles of the slippery material together on an old hand-operated Singer sewing machine and finished the job as dawn was breaking. No complaints and no hassles. If you asked her to cook, she'd cook. Do reservations, she'd do it. Deliver a baby. She'd do it. She also takes decisions quickly and when she puts her mind to something she not only does the job but does it superlatively. Both Shan and Dave have a good balance in their lives. They take the tough times in their stride and enjoy the fun and the glamour of life at Londolozi." The Shangaan community have given Shan a title of utmost respect. They call her 'Ndlovukazi' – the mother elephant.

Yvonne Short, who with her husband Peter took over as a team managing the camps, had many experiences with elephants which used to visit them each winter. Pete, coming home late after the last guests had left the boma, would often find elephants in his front garden and have to creep into his house like a burglar through the bathroom window. The rule was – don't invade their territory and they will leave you alone. "We were convinced one elephant always waited for us behind the kitchen wall," says Yvonne. "As soon as we loaded the lunch onto the Land Rover to be delivered to the other camps less than a kilometre away, he would snaffle the salad and be off – only to appear at the same time the next day."

One young catering assistant had a rather hair-raising introduction to Londolozi. "It was almost enough to make her pick up her bags and leave even before they were unpacked," said Yvonne. On her first day, she had the task of delivering lunch from the main kitchen to the two satellite camps. Somehow or other she managed to get off in a rush before the elephant got to the lettuce. He was not impressed and gave a mock charge. Round the next bend she saw a little duiker in the road and as she approached a leopard came out of the bush and took the duiker right in front of her! "After that first day," said Yvonne, "it took a lot of talking to persuade her to stay."

Yvonne, who was in charge of hospitality at Londolozi before being promoted to group hospitality manager with Conservation Corporation, spares no effort to make every day unique for guests. A birthday or an anniversary is a good reason for a special occasion. So is a full moon, the first summer rains, the birth of leopard cubs or the sighting of buffalo and elephants that have crossed the old fence line and arrived in the Sabi Sand. "We make the most of our weather by arranging bush dinners throughout summer for all our guests," says Yvonne. But for sheer romance, a dinner *tête-à-tête* in the Londolozi bushveld is a never-to-be-forgotten experience.

Driving to one of these bush dinners and towards the sound of African drums is full of excitement. On the way there could be a few hyena anticipating the titbits that may be left behind. The log fire in the middle of the clearing is surrounded by hundreds of flickering lights – on the ground, in the trees and on the tables. It looks like fairyland. Everything is exquisitely set out. It is an enormous amount of work. Yvonne recounts the occasion after a particularly hot dry summer's day: "It was a lovely evening with the sparkling African sky and the moon just rising above the horizon. We were relaxing, patting ourselves on the back because this time we could draw breath before our guests arrived. Then pandemonium erupted. A herd of wildebeest hotly pursued by a pride of lions literally flew straight past us and through the clearing leaving dust and broken crockery and glass in their wake – and a very rattled catering staff!"

The real significance of what 'belonging to Londolozi' meant, was brought

Duiker, seemingly vulnerable to the predation of eagles, snakes and carnivores, manage to survive by being largely nocturnal and well hidden in dense bush. They are usually found singly, or during the mating season, in pairs.

Opposite: Life at Londolozi revolves around the wildlife; elephants in your garden are treated with respect and left to their own devices, even if they push down your favourite tree. Animals always have priority.

Next pages: Driving to a bush dinner at Londolozi one may see a pride of lions and many smaller nocturnal creatures: a pearlspotted owl whose oversized talons belie its meek appearance, a thick-tailed bushbaby which will leap from branch to branch when disturbed, an African civet and a large-spotted genet, two of the smaller but formidable carnivores seldom seen during the day at Londolozi.

Above: A baby impala's curiosity is whetted by two dung beetles having a dispute over a ball of dung, and John's dog 'Tiger'. Lions killed an impala right against their prefab wall. Tiger ran out and started to bark at the lions but when they turned around Tiger turned tail and fled, first knocking out the paraffin lamp and then knocking down the lean-to door to the hut. John grabbed a blanket for protection but the next minute in the pitch dark an animal landed on top of him. For a few seconds he didn't know whether it was 'Tiger' or a lion. The next day they found tracks right to the door but the lioness had turned back to eat the impala.

Opposite: Dave, Shan, Bronwyn and Boyd.

home to Yvonne and Peter with the loss of their 17-month-old twin daughter in 1993. Yvonne talks with tears in her eyes of the support she and Pete received from everyone. Shan chartered a plane from Johannesburg and was at the Nelspruit hospital even before they arrived. Dave was overseas and called every single day. JV was in the middle of filming, but put aside time just to sit with them. The love and caring that came from the community they worked with was beyond anything Yvonne had ever experienced. "We may have heard a rustle, nothing more. In true Shangaan tradition, every evening 70 or 80 people came and sat quietly in our garden, sharing our sorrow and comforting us. Sometimes they would pray, sometimes they would sing a hymn." After the funeral the community made a collection and bought a tree in memory of the little girl who had died. It still grows in their garden.

This was an example of the remarkable group consciousness or ubuntu that developed at Londolozi. Ubuntu – a word taken from the Zulu language – is often heard and practised at Londolozi. There is no word in the English language that completely describes ubuntu. It is the combination of a good moral disposition, of thoughtfulness, kindness, generosity and hospitality. A Zulu may say *"Wo, akumuntu lowo"* (He is no person) if he does not display ubuntu.

Yvonne herself is a brilliant teacher able to create enthusiasm, impart new ideas and direct her colleagues with wit and humour. She represents a new breed of professional women contributing significantly to Africa's ecotourism industry and making it globally competitive. "Everyone who comes to work at Londolozi is made to feel part of an inter-dependent 'family' group," says Yvonne. "It starts with Dave. He has a very special ability to communicate with people. You only have to see how the Shangaan people respect his 'straight talk' to know that Dave is special. Somehow he manages to put himself in other people's shoes. When he tells us of changes, he also gives us the reasons why. He sometimes takes us all down to the river and he shares his ideas and thoughts with us and afterwards we have a great celebration."

Not in the job description, the group of Londolozi extroverts has refined after-hours partying to a highly skilled art form. Parties, for staff birthdays and for the departure of a member of the 'family' group, often have a theme and it sometimes takes hours to prepare their dress. The result is that parties never get underway until after midnight. The ethic is you can party as late as you like but at dawn you have to be bright-eyed and bushy-tailed. "There was a great party for the launch of Lex's book *The Leopards of Londolozi*," says Yvonne. "Everyone was dressed in black and wore 'leopard' ears. When we heard two lions roar outside the boma we thought someone was playing a trick on us. But Trish who had gone to fetch something from the curio shop saw the lions through the door of the reception office. It was amazing timing. Fortunately after roaring at their reflections in the glass door, they went on their way."

Trish and James Marshall met at Londolozi and celebrated their marriage 'on the rocks' of the Sand river.

Wild pear blossoms (*Dombeya rotundifolia*); bushveld flowers fit for a bride.

Highly toxic seeds of *Abrus precatorius.*

What about after the parties? It would be hard to imagine a group of good-looking young, extrovert and healthy men and women put together in an isolated community not having fun in bed. The men, with JV as a role model, were the epitome of masculinity, the girls full of warmth and the promise of love. Sex was part of life at Londolozi but as one receptionist coyly commented: "You could always say no!" The isolation of the staff and the way they got to know each other had another effect. They learnt respect and they learnt love. The result was that over the past 15 years there were many serious romances and over 20 marriages between rangers and the girls in the camps – quite a high number considering that many of the staff were married before they arrived. Many marvellous wedding ceremonies took place 'on the rocks' on the bank of the Sand river opposite Main Camp. Trish and James Marshall, Ken and Lynn Maggs and Lex and Lynn Hes were three couples who started their married life there and it would be hard to imagine a more romantic setting, nor more happy and successful marriages.

Bush catering requires far more than normal culinary skills. It requires an immense ability to improvise and to adapt to any given situation. Once when Londolozi hosted a party of tribal leaders from the neighbouring KaNgwane Yvonne had been told to expect 50 people for lunch. One-hundred-and-fifty arrived! Yvonne went back into the kitchen and said to her staff: "You remember that story in the bible about the loaves and the fishes ...."

From time to time the entire camp is taken over by a corporate party. "We had an 18-page fax from Jaguar, London," says Yvonne. "They were bringing an overseas party to Londolozi and wanted everything to be perfect. We had planned every detail and the timing down to the last second but what we had planned and what actually happened on that first day were two different things.

"The day started with a drizzle so the guests who were departing started out on their morning game drive two hours late at eight o'clock. Straight away I knew we had problems," said Yvonne. "We had been asked to have all the rooms ready by eleven when the Jaguar party was due to arrive. We also had to have all their luggage (which was coming on an earlier plane) in their rooms so we'd look the swish operation everyone expected. We did all we could but we couldn't get into the rooms until our guests returned from their game drive – and of course they wanted breakfast before they packed up. We had a wonderful reception planned at the airstrip. First there would be iced champagne, then the Shangaan women would dance and finally all the rangers were to drive in an impressive convoy over the hill and up the runway to greet the guests. I had sent a ranger, who had recently arrived at Londolozi, ahead to set up trestle tables for the champagne at the airstrip and had briefed the dancing ladies to drop their work and come to the airstrip the minute they heard the aircraft overhead. The rangers were to follow 15 minutes later.

"When I got to the top of the hill I found to my horror all three aircraft circling overhead and unable to land. Our diligent young ranger had set up the tables and champagne, all beautifully set out, on the runway! The panic was on. We quickly dismantled the tables rushing backwards and forwards in the Land Rover, resetting everything under a tree while the aircraft came down one by one. In the rush I didn't notice that the hand brake of the Land Rover had been on all the time until I smelt something burning. We had started a bush fire and the only liquid we had to douse the flames was champagne. So we popped corks and smothered the fire as best we could, but not before we had a very black and burnt reception area and a half-burnt-out Land Rover. We had no option but to greet our very important guests with smutty noses and rather wry smiles." So much for planning!

"When Shan took up flying," Dave says, "I had no option but to renew my licence. If there is ever a way to test and to cement a marriage it is flying together. We sold our Range Rover for R57 000 and bought our first Cessna 182 for R58 000. We called ourselves the 'White-knuckle Charter Company'. You could cut the tension with a knife during those first 150 hours. The children were told to get into flying mode. No games. No talking.

"We had very strict rules. We flew leg for leg. Whoever was the passenger was not allowed to criticise the pilot while in the air. We would check the weather with the met office and then phone Sonja, owner of a Wimpy Bar at Belfast, the highest point on our flight between Johannesburg and Londolozi. If she said: 'Daar is geen wolke nie, Dawie,' (there are no clouds) we'd take off. We had our differences on flying techniques but I really was proud of Shan. It was such a common bond and we never for a moment ever ran out of conversation. We flew together all over southern Africa as well as ferrying back and forth from Londolozi to Johannesburg. We even used the aircraft to take building materials into Ngala, the Conservation Corporation lodge north of Londolozi, when it was under construction. We had a few accidents. Fortunately none were serious. Mostly they were caused by our inexperience."

Flying added another dimension to Shan's life which had already been so full. How many people have the opportunity to experience Austria on $7 a day and then return like Cinderella to be fêted at a glittering Viennese ball for members of Relais et Chateaux? How many collect herbs with Shangaan women and dance with the Masai after a day ballooning over the Masai Mara? How many are introduced to zebroids and the almost extinct bongo only found in the mountains of central Africa? How many enjoy a fabulous picnic on the Ngorongoro crater floor, with a spectacular thunderstorm on one side of the crater and an equally magnificent rainbow on the other? How many have been to the Secret Place of the Elephant in Damaraland? Flown around Mt. Kenya in a Piper Cub? Visited the Cannes film festival? Seen a pennantwinged nightjar? But then

Fires often start naturally in the bushveld. The summer storms, accompanied by lightning, will spark a fire that may run over wide areas before being put out by a rainstorm.

Above: *Urginea sp.* and below, *Aptosimum indivisum*, flower after spring rains on the Londolozi airstrip.

One night Shan went into the store-room without a lamp but knowing exactly where to find the bottle of wine she needed. Instead she grasped a python.

Opposite: Another of Shan's experiences was being charged by an elephant.

Below: Londolozi became the regular meeting place for Bobby Lawrence, Enos Mabuza, John and Dave to discuss conservation and the formation of the Songimvelo game reserve in KaNgwane. The bronze casting of three buffalo known as the Nyati Pack, which stands at Londolozi's Main Camp entrance and was sculpted by Bobby, is symbolic of the friendship between these men.

how many women learn to fly? How many become a presenter of a Disney video series? How many become a director of an international wildlife company and expert in human resources – so much so that they are able to set up their own personnel business? And how many still have time to devote love, time and attention to two children and then still time to give so much caring to so many people? Shan does all of that and so much more.

"Life with Dave and belonging to Londolozi has been extraordinarily special," says Shan. "I've had the most wonderful opportunities and experiences, although some preferably not to be repeated; like being stung by a scorpion, putting my hand on a python, being charged by an elephant, chased by lion, nearly cycling over a black mamba and having to yank my sister's front teeth back into their sockets when a branch whiplashed across her face!

"I have met many special people. Tina Turner gave a never-to-be-forgotten performance singing *Sometimes when we Touch* while lying on the bare ground of the boma next to the fire and under a canopy of stars. It was electrifying," says Shan. "Some Londolozi visitors are instantly recognisable, like John Major, Brooke Shields and Spike Milligan. Others were equally wonderful to have as guests and we made friends and stayed friends forever." Neil and Morag Hulett gave Shan and Dave their first lessons in sophisticated living and Bobby Lawrence and his wife Milly widened their circle of friends, introducing them to many American visitors and to people who would play a major role in conservation in South Africa in the years ahead.

A talented sculptor of wildlife, Bobby was fascinated by the Varty brothers' initiative. He had met a progressive young man in the Lowveld, Enos Mabuza, who worked as an inspector of schools and was interested in wildlife. Bobby introduced him to Dave and John and he spent many weekends visiting Londolozi and learning their philosophy. Enos went on to become Chief Minister of KaNgwane, a position he held for 13 years. During that time, in part influenced by their many discussions, Enos established four game reserves in the territory under his jurisdiction.

After Enos Mabuza retired from politics he was appointed to the National Parks Board and the following year, in 1995, he became chairman of the board, one of the most prestigious of all conservation appointments in South Africa. As a staunch supporter of the ANC, Enos had become a close friend of Nelson Mandela and Thabo Mbeki, deputy president of South Africa. At Enos's suggestion both visited Londolozi.

"Not long after Nelson Mandela made his legendary walk to freedom he made the first of several visits to Londolozi," says Shan. "It was a desperately dry summer. There was not a blade of grass and it was very, very hot – 35° in the shade. Dave had been to the neighbouring homeland that day to ask the Minister to release water dammed upstream on the Sand river so that we would

at least have some water downstream. He declined on the grounds that they needed the water for irrigation. Our hippo population was virtually gone. They had little time left to survive unless their pools were replenished. When Dave got back he found Nelson Mandela sitting on the verandah of John's house. Dave recounted what he had been doing that day and why there was no water in the river." Shan remembers Nelson Mandela's comment: "When we run this country we will not permit the river catchments to be abused. I promise you, we will bring appropriate management to the rivers." That night the drought broke and the river, which is only 70 kilometres from source to where it joins the Sabie river, came down in flood. There was huge excitement. "The next day John called a meeting in the village to give thanks for the rain. We all joined hands and participated in the communities' rain dance. Mr. Mandela addressed us. He has such a presence. It was an incredible privilege for all of us. He described to the people of Londolozi the harmony he felt amongst the different race groups and said that this represented his vision for the future of South Africa; good jobs, good quality of life and good education for the children.

"After he was elected president and addressed the Natal Parks Board, President Mandela referred to Londolozi as the role model for the future conservation development of South Africa. He also made good his promise and river management, under the direction of Kadar Asmal, Minister of Water Affairs and Forestry in the new government, has significantly improved."

Opposite: A greenbacked heron (*Butorides striatus*) flying above the silt-laden Sand river.

Feathers from two birds often seen at Londolozi: the lilacbreasted roller, *Coracias caudata*, and the whitefronted bee-eater, *Merops bullockoides*.

WIDENING HORIZONS

If you can fill the unforgiving minute
with sixty seconds' worth of distance run,
Yours is the Earth and everything that's in it.
And – which is more – you'll be a Man, my son!
— *Rudyard Kipling*.

F THERE WAS ONE COMMON THREAD that linked the various stages of JV's life together, it was the passion with which he tackled everything. Head boy of his school, provincial cricketer, tenacious hunter, achieving his university degree while developing a successful business against all odds, and pioneering bush clearing which turned Londolozi into a magical wildlife habitat. JV had grown up in an environment in which facing challenges was second nature and he had thrived at every hurdle. Londolozi had been a steep learning curve but after a decade of incredibly hard work, he decided to take some time off and leave Londolozi to Dave and Shan.

In 1981, travelling on a South African passport, which in those days was virtually a passport to nowhere, JV managed to get into Kenya – although not without spending three days in jail. He then joined a Kenyan anti-poaching unit for about nine months and had unique opportunities to see the country. One day he was questioned by the Kenyan police who wanted to know his rank in the unit. It was tactfully suggested that he had better disappear quickly. He spent the next two months with legendary George Adamson in the remote Northern Frontier District of Kenya before flying across the border and back to Londolozi.

Already new ideas were starting to take shape. He had frequently been asked to advise wildlife film-makers and began to appreciate the power of electronic media to reach millions of people. JV saw a new role for himself with new challenges: that of being a global communicator through film and television. In some ways the step was not great, it was a natural extension of his Londolozi activities. In the early days he had led wilderness trails, going out into the bush for five days at a time with groups of teenagers, teaching them about wildlife and conservation. They would camp at various places along the Sand river and for a small sum (the trail's camps started at R3 a day) everyone would have a great time. Then as a ranger JV was always teaching, giving information, creating adventure and exciting the imagination of young people. With Elmon Mhlongo with whom he had formed a close friendship, they could track and find almost anything for their guests. You wanted a lion, you would get a whole pride. A leopard. They would find one. Elephants. They would be at the river. These weren't accidents. They were the products of a systematic search and careful observation. And you would learn all the time you were with him.

In Kenya JV saw for the first time a true wilderness with large herds of elephants and big prides of lions. He saw the vast grasslands of the Masai Mara, the venue of one of the greatest wildlife shows on earth – the wildebeest migration. JV realised how much more productive land in Africa could be without man's intervention; without development, fence lines and agriculture. He met David Hopcroft and George Adamson and began to learn from their wisdom and experience.

As a ranger JV had set incredibly high standards. Now as a film-maker he would be able to set down his visionary thinking onto film and reach millions of people all over the world. He appreciated there had been a global shift in man's conscious relationship with animals which had changed from the role of hunter to protector and he wanted to explore that relationship further. He was prepared to make entertaining films, to go in front of the camera himself if

Judas and Elmon illustrate the art of bow-and-arrow hunting during the filming of *The Crossover*. The documentary tells the story of the last of the hunter/gatherers in the bushveld. JV explains how these people survived, living in harmony with nature, taking only for their needs and never destroying. They ate mopane worms, borers, monitor lizards, tortoises, snakes and fruit. Almost anything was edible. Deep-fried mopane worms have become a western delicacy. Perhaps we still have much to learn! Below: Buffalo.

Right: Elmon Mhlongo started tracking at Londolozi in the 70s and ten years later he joined JV in film-making. He combines a superb ability to observe and listen with an intuitive understanding of wildlife.

necessary, all with one objective – to communicate his thinking about wildlife and conservation in an entertaining way to as many people as possible.

JV's best friend was, and still is, Elmon Mhlongo. Elmon had learnt the art of hunting and tracking from his father, Judas and his uncle, Engine Mhlongo, who was famous for his hunting skills. They were amongst the last bow-and-arrow hunters in the community. JV's deep friendship with Elmon was not compatible with the apartheid system and the hypocrisy that went hand in hand with it. He felt a compelling need to try and alter attitudes, especially those relating to the indigenous black people he had grown up with, and to conservation which was generally regarded as a poor cousin to industry.

The wilderness was considered neither to be of any economic significance nor of any serious aesthetic value. JV wanted to alter that perception. He believed that through film he could make people concerned about habitat destruction which was resulting in more and more species dying out every day. Perhaps he could help start a ground swell of opinion that might channel some of the spending on warfare – which at its peak had reached $1.2 million a minute worldwide – into conservation. Although in the long term JV believed that conservation tourism could provide the income to make the wilderness a self-sustaining business.

JV realised that he could communicate far more effectively with a camera in his hands. Besides, it also suited his personality. From the time of his father's death he had had little option but to override his natural introversion in order to achieve his goals. He valued space around him. In that respect he was not unlike the predators he had come to understand almost better than people. His territory was carefully guarded and few were allowed to cross into that very private inner circle while his ideas were as wide as the bushveld horizons. Shan describes JV as the most courageous person she has ever met when it comes to living life according to his own set of values, ethics and rules. If he did not comply with society, he said, stuff them! If he didn't have money, he found it and if he didn't have the knowledge he would go to any length to acquire it. The result had been an often misunderstood character but, by his thirtieth year, an incredible success story.

Anyone who thinks that the life JV then embarked on was one of glamour and excitement, has not held a film camera while following leopard through the dense African bush, a jaguar through the jungles of South America or a tiger in the foothills of the Himalayas. It is incredibly hard physical work and there is always the element of danger. JV calls himself an adventurer. And adventures he has had. He has escaped death too closely and too often not to value intensely every moment of his life. He has been charged by lion, even to the point of being knocked down. He narrowly escaped being gored by a buffalo. He just managed to side-step the vicious jaws of a crocodile on the banks of the

Above left: *Acacia nigrescens*, knob thorn.

Above right: *Acacia nilotica*, scented thorn.

Sand river when his attention was on filming giraffe on the opposite bank. He has been caught in a wildebeest and zebra migration in the Masai Mara and he has literally crawled away from a helicopter accident.

As a hunter and a ranger JV used his extraordinary tenacity to track and find animals. All his bush skills were only a beginning. In his thirst for knowledge, JV turned first to books to learn more about animal behaviour. He read all he could lay his hands on and has built up a substantial library. But it was not enough. It gave him only 30 percent of the knowledge he was after. He went back to George Adamson. Then he found a man who had spent 20 years working in a circus and was regarded as a genius with tigers. JV sat for two days in his caravan listening to him talk and playing with his tigers. With elephants, JV says, you get a whole new perspective when you talk to people who have spent 30 years working closely with them. You come to understand the nature of these intelligent massive beasts which not only share about the same life span as man, but also have a psyche not unlike our own. They have thoughts and feelings, they can play games, they have humour and can tease and even cheat, they can get annoyed and, they have the ability to love and to sorrow.

JV watched keepers in zoos and listened to their talks, sometimes to 500 people and more. He noted the interest in the interaction between man and animal. Altogether JV visited more than 25 zoos in the United States alone. It changed his views on animals in captivity. "Zoos have gone through their own evolution," says JV. "They've saved at least 15 animals from extinction and are starting to get them back into the wild; Arabian oryx, blackfooted ferret, red wolf, South American condor to name a few." Wherever he went he found people with unique and fascinating stories to tell and new perceptions about animals, particularly an awareness that there is an inter-species communication link. For JV this was just a beginning.

In his film-making he looked for a special niche in the market. He was hardly likely to be able to compete with the major BBC documentaries; he had to be different. More and more, as he developed his talent he found those productions that achieved the highest ratings involved both people and animals. Two of his films *Silent Hunter* and *Swift and Silent*, involved both Elmon and himself. The former is an in-depth story of a leopard, the latter compares the three great spotted predators, the jaguar, the leopard and the cheetah. JV made many other videos within these parameters. He told the story of the hunter/gatherers who live side by side with Africa's major predators, the lion, leopard and cheetah. He made a 52-part *Bush School* series presented by Shan. Six children, including Shan and Dave's two children, Bronwyn and Boyd, took part in this fascinating series commissioned by Walt Disney. "The series was great fun," says Shan. It was translated into many languages and shown in 19 countries to an estimated viewership of 50 million people. It also acted as a

Top: There are many aspects of an elephant's psyche to which we can relate but perhaps none more so than the mother's love and concern for her young – and the sheer exuberance and mischievousness of youth.

Above: Shan Varty and her team, Adam and Simon Bannister, Tidi and Sizi Modise and Bronwyn and Boyd Varty, who worked on Londolozi Production's extremely successful 52-part video series *Bush School* commissioned by Disney.

Opposite: One of the leopard at Londolozi climbs a tree to get a better view of his surroundings and possible prey.

JV and Gillian's daughter Savannah with Lakakin Sukuli who, with his brother Karino, participates in many of JV's Masai Mara film shoots. They are JV's partners in the cattle business which was the key to setting up a filming camp in Kenya. The Masai call Savannah 'Nashipia', happy one.

Masai earrings.

catalyst, igniting a wildlife interest in children across the world who identify with the kids in JV's programmes as well as with JV and Elmon. Combined with his depth of understanding of animals, this is what makes JV's productions so very different from many big budget wildlife films where the crews walk in, shoot and walk away.

JV's real strength is his ability to reach a unique cross-section of people. On the same day he would speak with the President of Zambia and with a poacher who has killed a thousand elephants or more. Both would tell their own stories. Over the years his productions have taken him all over the world and he has built up a network of contacts in Kenya, Tanzania, Zambia, Zimbabwe, South Africa, the United States, Canada, Australia, Peru and the Amazon. His circle of friends has grown so wide that he has started a newsletter to keep in touch with everyone.

His films have achieved top ratings on U.S. TV channels and have been seen by millions of people and, he hopes, have resulted in a greater reverence for our planet and all living things. He has won many top documentary honours such as the New York Gold Award, the Film Festival of Montana Best Independent Programme and American Cable TV's Ace Award. Major international customers include Walt Disney, The Discovery Channel, Time Life, Reader's Digest and Turner Original Programmes (TOP). Not bad for a camera team of JV and Elmon! Only recently he has expanded his base and now has seven cameramen – two in Kenya, one in Canada, two in South Africa and two following specific wildlife species in various parts of the world.

When JV first went hunting with a camera he was totally untrained in the art. He hadn't had a single day of photographic schooling. He shot thousands of feet: he had 10 000 portraits, hundreds of pictures of leopard walking, sitting, sleeping. He thought he was going to make a great leopard film. But he didn't have the cutaways, the angles and the close-ups which put together under the hand of an expert editor, make for the drama and excitement of film. He didn't even have a story line. JV still lets the script of a wildlife film evolve. He does not consider himself an artist or even a superb technician with a camera, but he is a very good storyteller and he uses the footage effectively to awaken interest amongst people worldwide.

JV's first films and videos were shot at Londolozi. He later realised that the Masai Mara in Kenya with its vast open grasslands gave him the opportunity to become globally competitive. JV had already learnt his lesson trying to gain entry to Kenya on a South African passport. But the allure of filming on those wide open grassy plains, with visibility extending hundreds of miles in all directions, was too strong. Once again his determination came to the fore. He went off to South America and arranged Paraguayan passports for his entire family: including Shan, Dave, Elmon and Gillian van Houten, the lovely, raven-haired TV news presenter who JV had planned to work with on a Gaia video series – and then fell for and asked her to share his life. (Gaia, the goddess of the earth in Greek mythology, was the name given to the living planet by the astronauts.)

The next step was to meet the Masai tribesmen and gain their agreement to setting up a camp. Using his knowledge and experience gained amongst the Shangaan communities adjacent to Londolozi and his natural ability to communicate with tribal people, JV proposed to the tribesmen that he should be their partner; that he would buy cows and they would look after them in return for which he would have a campsite. JV recalls that they deliberated for about three weeks before they finally struck a deal. Warren Samuels, who had worked closely with JV at Londolozi had been born in Kenya. Together with his wife Heather, they took over the running of JV's new camp in the Masai Mara. The experience Warren has gained working there has given him the opportunity to become one of the best high-action cameramen in the wildlife business.

The Masai instinctively distrust strangers. To break down this barrier and to build up a relationship with the Masai he adopted a favour-for-favour system and of course always stuck to his word. After he had bought five cows much goodwill grew out of the partnership and he has represented the Masai on committees trying to help them manage their land. He now owns quite a large herd. On one occasion the Masai brought a cow to his camp. He asked why and was told that one of their jointly-owned cows had been taken by a lion. JV tried to convince them that as they were in partnership, he would accept the loss. No, they said, the herdsman was asleep and it was their fault that the cow had been killed. It was their responsibility to replace it. JV invited his Masai partners to South Africa. They stayed at Londolozi and at Phinda near the Maputaland coast, where for the first time they saw the sea.

The power of JV's films as a marketing tool was brought home to Dave and Shan back at Londolozi. After dinner in the boma Dave asked their guests if they would like to see the video, *Silent Hunter*. No one expressed the slightest interest. Rather put out, Dave asked why. He soon discovered that everyone had seen the video. It had sparked a keen interest in the reserve. That's why they were at Londolozi. The same with the next group. And the next. Over and over again the entire camp was sold out because of the film. Right through the decade before South Africa's first democratic general election in 1994, many hotels ran at crippling occupancy rates of less than 20 percent. In contrast, Londolozi ran at an average of 80 percent. Londolozi Production's videos were reaching millions of people and those who could afford it wanted to see Londolozi for themselves.

Back at Londolozi JV, assisted by Gillian, began planning a major new venture, one he had dreamed about for years. JV never forgot the occasion

Top: Gillian takes a lesson in milking a cow. The Masai do not kill their cattle for meat, except for traditional ceremonies. Above: The Masai celebrate a wedding, a circumcision, a birth in the traditional 'dress' which characterises their tribe. Here Gillian is plastered with ochre-dust before a wedding ceremony.

A gourd in which the Masai combine milk and blood taken from their cattle.

Above: A young Thomson's gazelle and a baby zebra speak of the productivity and health of the land and of the survival of species.

Right: Little Boy and Little Girl, stars of the film *Running Wild*, who were successfully released in Zambia's Luangwa National Park by JV, Gillian and Elmon.

when the mother leopard had nearly been taken by a lion but, instinctively, abandoning his own rules and because he knew she had two six-week-old cubs, he had distracted the lion and the mother leopard escaped. JV felt that if she had been killed he would have rescued the helpless cubs. For years JV had built up material on the mother leopard. He wanted to do something bigger and better than the documentaries he had already made. It was part of his essential need to communicate. He planned to make the two orphaned cubs the main focus of his script. The story of JV and Gillian's production of *Running Wild* starring JV and Brooke Shields, and the release of the boy and girl leopards into the Luangwa valley, has been wonderfully told by Gillian both on video tape and in print.

Many people prophesied that the film would be a financial disaster. Peter Gallo who jointly underwrote the production is delighted with sales. "It has been sold into every major market in the world." Perhaps of even more significance to JV is that the film was seen by one of the most influential men in the electronic media industry, Ted Turner chief executive of CNN. When the film was being launched, the Turner group was completing market research into wildlife films. Just as JV had discovered a long time earlier, they found that interaction between people and animals created a far higher level of interest than classic wildlife documentaries. It was not long before a meeting was set up. By that time JV was in hospital recovering from his helicopter crash, but despite his pain and extreme discomfort he was aware that for the first time he would be meeting like-minded people. They too wanted to create hard-edged yet entertaining programmes with the purpose of making the world a better place.

While *Running Wild* was still in the planning stage, JV and Gillian came across a helpless lion cub abandoned by its mother at Londolozi. At the back of their minds they had already agonized over the rights and wrongs of interfering with nature by temporarily 'adopting' the leopard cubs. Perhaps ten years or even five years earlier JV would never have acted as he then did. Their reaction to this beautiful little cub was emotional and instinctive. They picked it up and saved it from certain death. "She would have been dead in a few hours," says JV. Two-and-a-half years later Shingalana, her life and her tragic death, have come to be one of the legends of Londolozi.

JV and Gillian had the choice of putting her in a zoo or taking the risk of preparing her for her release back into the wild, not a good situation for a single cub. They had hoped they would find another lion cub, which would have given Shingi a much better chance to survive but in the limited time they had, they were unable to find one. They decided to take a chance. In the end because Shingi was so imprinted on JV and Gillian and had never played with other lions, she didn't want to return to the wild, she wanted to stay with them. The leopard cubs had grown up together and had never identified with humans.

The remote Luangwa valley was ideal territory in many respects for the release of both the two leopard cubs and Shingalana. JV and Gillian had prepared all three to fend for themselves and the two leopard cubs were soon revelling in their freedom. For Shingalana, the valley was hostile. Two large prides had moved into the area, one of 11 lionesses and the second of 14. JV and Gillian spent a year watching Shingi accustom herself to her new territory. She had even mated. But the lionesses would not tolerate her presence and she died tragically one drama-filled night. JV wished he could have found an area with fewer lions which would have given her a better chance of surviving the difficult transition back into the wild.

Below: Fruit of the green monkey orange tree, *Strychnos spinosa*.

Left: Shingalana when she was abandoned by her mother and picked up by JV and Gillian at Londolozi.

Right: Shingalana growing up and with JV and with Gillian.

John's Masai bangle.

Top: The Ngorongoro crater in Tanzania, 20 kilometres across and 700 metres deep, provides a wonderful haven for zebra. Above: The olive baboon found in Kenya is too formidable an adversary for most leopards. In comparison the smaller yellow baboon found in the Luangwa valley is vulnerable to both leopard and the smaller carnivores.

Opposite: The fruit of two strong creepers which are found trailing over bushveld trees, the spiky fruit of the *Cucumis metuliferus* and the large round fruit of *Lagenaria mascarena*.

Their return to the wild was a success. Within a week they had disappeared into the Luangwa valley in Zambia, leaving their year of filming and JV, Gillian and Elmon behind. Shingi was different.

"She had a wonderful character," Gillian remembers. "She was gentle, affectionate, playful – and had a great sense of humour – even wicked at times but never malicious." For over 30 months they lived an isolated life at the Shingalana camp at Londolozi. During the year the leopard cubs were with them they divided their time between two camps, one for Shingi and the second, a treehouse for the leopard cubs. Once in the Luangwa valley the cubs were soon off their hands. But when JV and Gillian were preparing Shingi for her release, time and time again she would return to their base camp, even when she was associating with the males in the area and had mated with one of them. They thought she was well on the road to independence. Then one night a pride of lionesses, who had realised she was permanently living in their territory, attacked and killed her. It was like losing a child they had loved dearly, yet it was not, partly because it was a very private grief. Theirs had been an extraordinary and very special relationship. It was devastating for both of them.

Right at the outset JV knew the problems that he and Gillian would encounter and the criticism that they would have to face because they had interfered with nature. When they launched the video on Shingalana, the criticisms came – mostly from the scientific and academic fields. The press were particularly vicious. There was also a tidal wave of positive response, largely because many people could relate to JV, Elmon and Gillian's involvement. Children particularly, unfettered by scientific thinking, had a far greater empathy with the planet's creatures and loved the story of the lioness. The video on Shingalana, in its first year, was shown in 30 countries and people all over the world talked about her. JV and Gillian also added significantly to the knowledge available on lion behaviour.

A few months after JV and Gillian's daughter, Savannah, was born in March 1995, JV was filming – again in the Luangwa valley. Every moment of that day is imprinted in his memory. The morning had been successful. They had discovered a large herd of buffalo moving through the mopane forest but the clouds had come up and they decided to abandon filming for the day. Back at camp on the Luangwa river JV discussed flying techniques with the pilot, Rob Parsons. JV had an idea to create a mobile flying hospital for people and for animals in remote areas such as where they were in Zambia. He had already accumulated 40 hours of helicopter flying time and was taking an ambulance course to learn more about injuries.

At about four o'clock the clouds lifted and the light was very beautiful so they decided to go back to film the buffalo. "There were five of us in the helicopter," recalls JV. "Rob was piloting, I was next to him. Karen Slater, William

Sabonya and Elmon Mhlongo were in the back. Because we knew where the herd was we did not climb to our normal 2500 feet. We stayed just above the trees at about 400 feet. That was an amazing bit of luck for us. Suddenly we heard a sharp crack and the helicopter shuddered. My first thought was that poachers had shot us from the ground.

"The next second the helicopter started to spin and we knew we had lost the tail rotor – a pilot's worst nightmare. Rob was a brilliant pilot. In the 25 seconds we had before we hit the ground he had switched off the engine and cut the fuel – which saved us from going up in flames. He also managed to keep the helicopter level while we were spinning and to manoeuvre the machine between two mopane trees. An almost impossible task. We must have missed the big tree on our right by six inches. It would have turned us over.

"Elmon, who had wanted to jump before we hit the ground, had been persuaded by William to get back into his seat. 'If we die, we die with Makho-khwana (JV's Shangaan name),' he said. William shoved his belt back on seconds before we hit the ground. Both were physically stable but in shock. I managed to crawl out. Amazingly Karen walked away from the crash and then went back to help William. Rob was trapped in the cockpit and was in considerable distress. With my limited medical knowledge I decided he was better off where he was and told him that he would be a paraplegic if we tried to drag him out of the cockpit." JV could neither stand nor walk. He had broken vertebrae but he could feel his toes.

"Karen was fantastic and very courageous," he recalls "I gave her a gun and told her to walk to the river, turn right and she would reach our camp. She had less than three hours to get there to be able to pick up our seven o'clock fixed-time radio call to civilization. She not only made it back to the camp walking through one of the wildest valleys in southern Africa, she also arrived in time to send the message out to JV's Lusaka agent, Yusef Patel."

Trish Parsons, Rob's wife, and JV's game scouts left immediately walking in the dark to be first on the scene of the accident. JV had told Karen that they should fire their guns when they got into the vicinity of the crash. JV answered with his revolver and very soon the scouts located them. The first thing he did was to instruct the four scouts how to extricate Rob from the cockpit. "I threatened them that if they did not follow my instructions to the letter I was going to shoot them," said JV. "You've never seen four guys lift anybody so carefully!" Later the x-rays of his spinal column showed Rob was millimetres away from being a paraplegic.

Loyd Gumede, one of JV's scouts, crossed the Luangwa river at midnight to ask for help at another camp. John Knowles, a former Londolozi ranger came to assist them, wading across the river which was waist deep, full of crocodiles and incredibly dangerous. Loyd returned with him. The loyalty, support and

Overleaf: John Varty filming from a helicopter in the remote Luangwa valley.

Above: The Luangwa valley is distinctly unsuitable to wander through alone and at night as Karen Slater did when she returned to camp to fetch help for her injured friends. The valley is filled with huge herds of buffalo and elephants and the river has an abundance of hippo and crocodiles.

Traditional Masai regalia.

courage which they showed was far beyond anything that could be expected. Karen, who had fractured vertebrae, courageously walked back at first light to see if she could help.

Karen's message reverberated quickly to South Africa and eventually to Dave and Shan who were holding a management conference at the Blue Mountain Lodge in the eastern Transvaal. They got up from the dinner table and simply never went back. Dave was busy mobilising two Citation jets to Mfuwe, the nearest runway to the accident and organising MRI – the South African Medical Rescue team – who took off from Johannesburg's international airport for Lusaka within hours. Yusef Patel had a busy night. After getting hold of Dave, he had to make contact with the Minister of Tourism and get the Lusaka airport reopened. The MRI team landed at four in the morning. In the meantime Dave and Yusef had been busy lining up a Zambian military helicopter and a spotter chopper which took off for the scene of the crash before first light. It took 14 long hours to position a qualified medical team at the scene of the crash. Soon thereafter all five were flown back to Johannesburg, Rob and JV into intensive care while Karen, William and Elmon were treated for shock and less severe injuries. Rob was pulled back from death's door about three times before he started on a long road to recovery.

During his six weeks in hospital JV was strapped into his bed and literally could not move. Some of his frustration at being in such an unusual situation was alleviated by a visit from Pat Mitchell, president of Turner Original Productions. He also started to get to know his lovely little blue-eyed daughter who has totally and unequivocally captured his heart – and who thought that all fathers spent their days in bed with only one mission in life, to entertain little girls!

Few people would take on the scope of the projects that JV tackles – with the potential for success but also for disaster. As soon as he was out of hospital JV was planning the next exciting chapter in his life. Developing ideas for two productions commissioned by the Turner Group and for a special production on the life of Elmon Mhlongo. Then he and Gillian were off to Kenya to meet up with their Masai friends, to the Bahamas, the United States and Canada filming about 20 different species in the snow, in forests and on the open plains.

Filming has done two things for JV. Firstly it has opened doors all over the world for him. "It is immensely helpful to be recognised by airline staff when you are carrying hundreds of kilograms of excess baggage," says JV. Many of the Delta and American Airlines' ground staff have seen his films and videos. They also meet up in very strange places with people who recognise them instantly: in the Amazon by a group of American birdwatchers, in the Negev desert by two Israeli scientists working on leopard, and in the Masai Mara after an enterprising man had put a portable video player on the back of a truck and shown JV's videos all over Kenya.

Secondly, it has broadened his horizons to the ecological disasters that man perpetrates globally. Visiting the Everglades for the first time, JV saw huge motorways and canals, armies of tractors and crop sprayers, and all the wonderful wildlife disappearing under the onslaught of man's insatiable demands. "It's exactly what could happen in the Okavango and is what is now happening in the bushveld," says JV. "There's only one way to stop an eventual eastern Transvaal desert and that is for us to look after our rivers and not to think they have an infinite capacity for abuse."

Ted Turner was influenced by one of the first films JV ever worked on. It was called *The End of Eden* and showed the destruction of habitat through overgrazing. As a result of that film Turner bought huge tracts of land in Montana where he replaced cattle with bison. "This is what we should be doing in Africa," says JV, "farming our most natural and valuable asset, our wildlife, not cattle and exotic trees that damage and drain our land."

It's hard to imagine Londolozi as a desert. But that's what could happen. One wonderfully wet summer can all too easily be followed by a decade of drought – we've seen the pattern time and time again over the past hundred years. JV describes the ecology of the Sabi Sand as fragile. The seeplines are small and dry out quickly. Not like the vast Serengeti and Masai Mara grasslands which are both massive sponge areas or seeplines.

Londolozi is fragile and very precious. If it's within JV's powers, he will do all he can to protect that magical place.

The long-necked gerenuk is perfectly adapted to making the most of the sparse vegetation of the dry northern areas of Kenya and Somalia.

THE DEVELOPMENT OF THE MODEL

Kakundlovu yasindwa sikhumba sayo
No elephant ever found its skin too heavy.
(There are always ways of managing one's problems.)
— *Zulu proverb.*

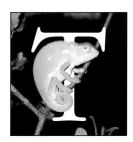

HE SAND RIVER FLOWS through Londolozi for about nine kilometres before continuing on its way through the Sabi Sand Wildtuin and to the Kruger National Park border where it joins the Sabie river. At times the river tumbles noisily over rocks and little waterfalls. Sometimes it spreads out wide, meandering slowly through shallow pools from which hippo eye one suspiciously, the sandy banks an open invitation to crocodiles which like nothing better than to bask in the sun. Around another bend the river is constricted between steep banks. Here wild sycamore trees with their gnarled roots overhang deep pools where kingfishers and fish eagles swoop to catch fish.

In a tree close to water hamerkop have made a huge nest. African folklore tells that there was once a prince and princess who belonged to two warring tribes. Forbidden ever to seal their love, they jumped from a high cliff into the river below. As they fell the gods took pity on them and changed them into birds, but doomed them forever to build bigger and bigger nests. Perhaps that is why their nests weigh up to 50 kilograms. Barn owls, giant eagle owls, martial eagles, pythons and mambas have been known to move into hamerkop nests almost as soon as they are completed. And the birds start again, forever building.

Londolozi's three camps have many similarities with hamerkop nests. They overlook water and make use of the huge jackalberry trees that grow along the banks of the river. Grass is used to make the lovely thatched rooftops of the camp buildings which blend into the surrounding bush just as well as the birds' nests. Londolozi's three camps have also undergone many changes since those early years and have been pulled down and rebuilt several times, emerging in 1997 full of charm and comfort.

Main Camp is exactly where Frank Unger and Charles Varty first pitched their tent on the banks of the Sand river. The boma fire has burnt on the same spot there for 70 years. The original four rondavels, no longer used for guests' accommodation, contain historic records of a past era and a future vision for conservation development in Africa. Today comfortable chalets each with their own river view give guests the privacy, peace and quiet that is part of the magical experience of Londolozi. The two satellite camps, Bush Camp and Tree Camp, the first safari camps to be recognised by Relais & Chateaux, are less than a kilometre east and west along the river. All three camps have been built to create an atmosphere of living close to nature. Each has an elevated deck overlooking the Sand river from where animals can be observed coming down to the river to drink and where many of the 300 different bird species in the Sabi Sand are to be seen. The soaring thatched roof of the main lounge and leisure deck at each of the camps gives protection against rain but never inhibits the feeling of the wide open space around you.

Above, a hamerkop flying over the Sand river and its huge nest, and below water-lilies flower on the dam near Main Camp. Opposite: A leopard at the Sand river.

Close your eyes and let the sounds of the bushveld create a picture of their own: wind rustling through the jackalberry trees, water cascading over the rocks, a fish eagle crying from across the river with its hauntingly beautiful song. Close by monkeys, always the opportunists, scamper and chatter about in the hope of some titbit or, in the author's own experience, to make off with a shiny Parker pen left unattended on the breakfast table.

Each camp has been deliberately kept small, partly to reduce the impact on the environment but also to give guests the opportunity to enjoy a degree of privacy and freedom seldom found in our modern world. Main Camp accommodates 20 people, Bush Camp 16 and Tree Camp 12; a total of 48 guests in 15 000 hectares of wilderness. To give some scale of population density; Greater London covers 150 000 hectares and contains some eight million people.

"Bush Camp," Dave says, "was initially built on the smell of an oil rag. It consisted of four mud huts with chicken mesh windows, corrugated iron roofs and wine boxes for shelving. But it had a magnificent position on the Sand river about a kilometre upstream from Main Camp. It was on land owned by Betty Taylor who had inherited the western half of Sparta from her father Frank Unger. Mrs. Taylor, who lived in Australia, agreed the small rental of R1 a day for each visitor who stayed in the camp. It was all we could afford.

"In the early 1980s we decided we should upgrade Bush Camp and were able to discuss our proposals first hand with Mrs. Taylor who was back in South Africa visiting her son Allan. While she was in South Africa she received numerous offers for her portion of Sparta. Once again it was crisis time for us. We were not in a position to compete. Years before we had started a camp without direct access from our own lands. We had even tried flying in but in the end we had to close the camp down. If Mrs. Taylor had sold the western portion of Sparta it would have left us high and dry.

"The situation came to a head at a meeting with Betty Taylor who was accompanied by Allan. There seemed to be every likelihood that the land would be lost to us but almost as the meeting ended and we thought we had lost out, Allan, who hadn't said a word the entire meeting spoke: 'I think we should stay with the Vartys,' he said. 'The Varty and Taylor families have been together for a long time. There's a tradition involved. Our grandfathers came here together. I think we should stick together.' There was a hushed silence and then Betty replied. 'Well Allan, ultimately it's going to be your property. If you believe in tradition beyond financial security that's what we'll do.'

"That's how our relationship with Allan began," says Dave. "We rebuilt Bush Camp and made it remarkably lovely. More importantly we found a friend and a true partner. Allan has been with us through thick and thin ever since." Allan, who had followed in his grandfather's footsteps, threw up his career as a mining engineer, pitched a tent on the Sand river and started to build a house for himself. He now lives in Cape Town and has developed a second career in computers but he visits Londolozi regularly and takes a keen interest in promoting the interests of the communities on the western border. "Allan and I are the same age and we share a common vision for Londolozi," says Dave. "We would like to keep it intact for our children. We hope when their turn comes, they will do the same."

By 1985 game viewing at Londolozi was exciting, probably the best in southern Africa, but the camps, while comfortable, were far from luxurious and the meals, while satisfying a healthy appetite, would not have excited the sophisticated tastebuds of a gourmet. While on marketing trips, Shan met two husband and wife teams who were to influence the development of Londolozi. Barbara and Rupert Jeffries had established the lovely Cybele Forest Lodge in the eastern Transvaal, the first hotel in South Africa to receive Relais & Chateaux status. Steve and Nicky Fitzgerald founded the exclusive Arniston Hotel on the southernmost tip of the African continent and were to make The Bay and Blues restaurant on the Cape peninsula, the superb operations they are today. Both the Jeffries and the Fitzgeralds became good friends of Shan and Dave.

At Cybele Shan noted the attention to detail and the quality of everything from the pure cotton sheets and down pillows to the fine cutlery and crockery. She also became aware of the superb service. Steve, who doesn't mince his words, voiced his opinion of Londolozi to Shan. "When you have the best safari operation in southern Africa, why is your hotel lousy?" Dave and John were not convinced. They were in the business of conservation, not hospitality. Shan thought otherwise. Steve's words really got her into gear.

In a relatively short time a plan for Tree Camp was drawn in the sand. And Shan discovered a formula for the decor which she has perfected to an art form; the use of the colours of the earth, the use of texture and the use of African artefacts and designs. The result is an interior that perfectly blends with and complements nature. Tree Camp was opened in 1986. It was an extraordinary leap of faith to commit expenditure of almost all they possessed to take Londolozi into the super class of the ecotourism industry, at a time when South Africa was digging an economic grave for itself by continuing along the path of apartheid. Dave and Shan, however, never for a moment doubted that South Africa would not find a solution to its ills. With its care of the land and wildlife in place Londolozi now planned to make caring of guests a top priority. Dave recognised that this could create a strong financial model with the potential to achieve his personal target: to make the game reserve economically viable and sustainably productive.

One thing was missing. Steuart Pennington who first visited Londolozi in the early 80s was quick to observe a weakness. He was one of a new generation of human resource professionals already planning for a future after the end of

Above: Allan Taylor, grandson of Frank Unger, with his children Anton and Kathleen. Below: Bronwyn and Boyd Varty are fascinated with the biodiversity of species at Londolozi which includes a lovely array of butterflies and dragonflies.

Opposite: On the leisure deck the cry of an African fish eagle is frequently heard while the crack of a twig announces the presence of an nyala which has found a relatively safe haven to browse. The sounds of the African bush create a symphony so completely in harmony that mechanical noise, which we listen to day in and day out for most of our lives, is so out of place, it offends the ear.

Above: In the evening the sounds of the wild carry for great distances while sometimes close by strange and startling sounds reach the ear. The sharp trumpet of an angry elephant and the contented vocal rumblings when they communicate and which may be heard at close range, all add to the African symphony.

Opposite: Top left, Ronnie McKelvey, general manager of Londolozi for nearly 10 years, together with Welding Mhlongo and Bishop Siwela, greet guests at the entrance to Main Camp.

Top right, Dave, Shan and Tony Adams with members of the staff and some of Londolozi's bush babies.

Below left, Shan and Siphiwe Ubisi, Londolozi's nursing sister.

Below right, as many of the staff as could be spared from essential services gather together on the rocks below Bush Camp.

apartheid. Steuart said that the Londolozi model was flawed and would fail unless the human dynamic was fully understood. A decade ahead of the reconstruction and development plan proposed by President Mandela, Steuart set about guiding Londolozi into a new employer/employee relationship which involved worker empowerment and participative management. Dave and Shan worked with Steuart adapting his urban human resource formula to a rural community and setting standards that would become the ecotourism industry's benchmark. He told them not to wait for a revolution but to become pro-active in laying down the ground rules for opportunity and job satisfaction. Their philosophy has resulted in an incredibly happy and unified team of people. Together they also established a professional human resource programme which would bridge the quantum gap from the small entrepreneur-managed operation at Londolozi into the global arena of Conservation Corporation.

Implementing Steuart's proposals was no quick-fix operation. It took three years of dedicated work to develop an understanding with their staff that apartheid was dead at Londolozi and that everyone should work shoulder to shoulder for the good of the game reserve, the guests and ultimately for themselves. The concept of ubuntu, of treating others as you would have them treat you and which has always been part of African culture, now came to the fore. Ubuntu led the way for the growth of a wonderful group awareness in which everyone supports each other. Another effect of changed attitudes was that instead of condoning rhino poaching, when their staff heard whispers of poaching activities in their area, they recognised that it was an attack on their community and resources and they would report what they heard.

The process of change spearheaded by Dave and Shan completed the third element of the model which became the working ethic for Londolozi and later for Conservation Corporation:

"We aim to create a model in wise land management using the multi-disciplines of a natural system, integrating international travellers and rural people to their mutual benefit. Our primary objective is to demonstrate that wildlife can be used on a sustainable basis by all."

The vital factor in the model the Vartys had created was care of staff and of the local communities. The mutual interchange of resources had resulted in the building of a relationship of trust and respect between the local people and Londolozi. Work began on a major upgrade of the staff village. A pre-primary and primary school, a clinic with a fully trained nursing sister in attendance, a church, recreational club and co-operative shop (part owned by employees) were added and a programme of involving all staff in Londolozi's social activities was set in motion.

Tony Adams, who had joined Londolozi as a ranger, took over the community programme supported by a wonderful group of dedicated people.

Left: Tree and Bush Camp are small retreats that blend with their natural surroundings. Bush Camp's lounge and the deck at Tree Camp set up for lunch.

Above: A purplecrested lourie, *Tauraco porphyreolophus* with brilliant scarlet underwing, is one of the most striking birds of the bushveld.

Right: The Main Camp leisure deck hidden amongst the giant jackalberry trees and one of the secluded Bush Camp suites overlooking the Sand river.

Feathers from the purplecrested lourie.

Above: There was an occasion when a beautiful mother giraffe futilely attempted to protect her helpless calf from a pride of increasingly determined lions. In her efforts to protect her little calf, she eventually kicked it to death. The drama and the sadness witnessed by the guests affected everyone deeply.

Opposite: Soon after the spring rains wilde-beest are born in great numbers – nature's way of ensuring the survival of the species.

Bauhinia galpinii, Pride-of-De Kaap.

Solly Mohaule, later appointed Conservation Corporation's rural development officer, and Siphiwe Ubisi, Londolozi's nursing sister, played a key role in opening the door and facilitating communication with local communities. Another member of the team was Trish Marshall. She had seen a marketing video on Londolozi and was quietly determined that she was going to work there. She had already moved from her home in New Zealand to Sydney, Australia and after a series of letters and faxes, Dave and Shan realised they were dealing with an unusual woman and offered her a job provided she could make her own way to South Africa. She arrived penniless and with all her possessions in a rucksack. But she was thrilled to be in the African bush. Later she married Jimmy Marshall who started his career at Londolozi as a ranger.

Two other lovely young girls, Shan's sister BJ Watson and Mel Piëst, arrived at about the same time and were typical of the many people who worked at Londolozi. Both were passionate about the bushveld and were determined to escape from big city life which had dealt them a pretty rough hand early in their lives. Trish and BJ took over as receptionists while Mel initially filled the formidable role of housekeeper and ran the bar. Later she joined BJ on reception. It all sounds very simple. But it was much more than looking pretty behind a desk. Being a receptionist meant doing the book-keeping, attending to the radio, telephone and fax, managing the shop and at the same time caring for guests, anticipating their needs, and entertaining them. There was no such thing as a specific job, if something had to be done someone did it; there was no buck passing. They did everything from assisting in the kitchen to introducing computer systems. BJ was somewhat daunted when she took on the challenge of preparing that most delectable of desserts, a *croque-en-bouche*, a brave creation which collapsed in front of her guests. That was one thing she did not try again.

Part of their job, says BJ, was to help people understand both the beauty and the inevitable tragedy of nature. Watching a kill can be an emotional, traumatic and horrifying experience. Once a guest asked, one could say demanded, to see a kill. By sheer chance almost immediately on leaving camp he watched a lion tear the back legs off a squealing warthog. He came back humbled and very thoughtful. It was a levelling experience. Nature is about life and death, each creation is a joy, each death gives life and so the circle continues. There is time for caring for what is past but ultimately we should celebrate the joy of life so vividly portrayed in the Londolozi bushveld.

After a day of exciting game viewing, many an evening was spent around the camp fire with JV playing the guitar and Trish, Mel and BJ doing a song and dance routine. They alternatively described themselves as 'Bertha and the Boma Lizards' or the 'Disappointed Sisters'. With their warm, friendly personalities, they were irresistible. They would create magic around the boma fire and people's

Schotia brachypetala, the weeping boer-bean tree.

Above: Endless bush 'yarns' flow over dinner in the boma after an exciting day in Africa. Shan Varty at the Sand river.

Right: One of the Frenchmen from Relais noticed the 'brooch' Shan was wearing on her cream linen dress. "C'est très bien," he said as he bent down to admire it closely. Then the 'brooch' spread its wings and flew away. "Mon dieu, incroyable!" he exclaimed in his astonishment. It was not surprising he had mistaken the insect for a brooch; it was a beautiful buprestid beetle, commonly known as a jewel beetle.

reserves would soon break down. On one occasion BJ told a rather complicated story to 40 people. She had her audience hanging on every word. And then she forgot the punchline. It was all fun. If there was a celebration the champagne would flow. If it was a good party Dave would open a bottle of Tequila or Sambuca on the house. The camaraderie amongst staff and guests was unique even for the most well-versed traveller. This is the magic of Londolozi.

As Shan says, "Londolozi is a learning ground in understanding human nature, communicating with guests, anticipating their needs and caring for one's colleagues. Living so closely together, the Londolozi community get to know each others' strengths and weaknesses. They learn never to judge people by their flaws, only on the sum of their attributes." They also learnt how to accept responsibility, how to take decisions standing on their feet and when necessary to improvise. Their target was keeping guests happy.

On one occasion BJ made a small mistake on a bill. To compensate for the error she gave the guest a discount ten times the overcharge. She was sure she would be fired. But that guest has come back to Londolozi over and over again. There were other incidents with guests when staff had to act quickly without thought of the cost. Like the occasion when two Japanese gentlemen asked to be shown the Southern Cross while they were having pre-dinner drinks in the boma. One of the rangers took them into the adjoining garden to get a better view of the stars. Armed with a champagne glass in one hand and an impala sosati (kebab) in the other, they gazed at the heavens above. Then came disaster. To get a still better view, they both took one too many steps backwards – straight into the icy swimming-pool. Yvonne wasted no time. The shop was opened and the guests, who had only come for one night, were kitted out in dry khakis – with the compliments of Londolozi.

Shan, Trish, BJ and Mel took on the task of preparing Londolozi to meet the high standards specified by Relais. There was a check list of 235 different items. Peter Short upgraded the wine cellar. Yvonne revolutionised the cuisine. Shan headed up the team to bring Londolozi staff to a high level of service excellence. Tony comments that Dave was one of the best motivators you could find. He continually challenged everyone to become a super-achiever. His creed was 'nothing less than perfect'.

Towards the end of 1990 Shan felt they were ready to apply for Relais membership. Unfortunately that summer was one of the worst they had had for years. Hardly a drop of rain fell. Temperatures soared up into the 40s, the dams dried up, there was not a leaf on a tree, not a blade of grass, not a flower. It was impossible to keep anything chilled. Shan and Yvonne did all they could to make Londolozi special for the two Relais officials who visited them. But it was just too hot to be enjoyable and the place literally crawled with bugs. On their return to Paris they wrote to say that there would be two further unannounced

visits by Relais officials. Later that year Shan received a letter from Relais advising that their membership had been approved. That was some celebration!

This was a major step in putting Londolozi on the map internationally. Shan, Waynne McLintock and Hugh Marshall, who is now working for Conservation Corporation, actively marketed Londolozi in the U.K., lecturing to many audiences so as to get Londolozi better known. A few years later in competition with 64 entrants from around the world, Londolozi was named the 1992 winner of the British Airways' Tourism for Tomorrow award which is given each year to the destination seen to have made the most positive impact on the environment and on local people.

"Shan, when she gets into her marketing mode, is formidable," says Dave. "She can sell anything to anybody. Part of her ability is her wide knowledge of all aspects of the business. Part is her ability to communicate directly and sincerely and to win people over. And part is her incredible energy and attention to detail." Dave believes that Londolozi's success was not altogether John's vision, nor was it his ability to implement John's ideas. It was Shan with her attention to detail who ultimately made the difference.

Londolozi's model for sustainable conservation development had reached maturity and could be copied to advantage elsewhere in Africa. With good conservation practices and professional hotel management, and by linking international travellers to wildlife areas, they had proved that conservation development was economically viable. Regional economies could be stimulated, rural people could find opportunity for equity participation, business partnerships, employment and training, green frontiers could be advanced and the home range of African wildlife extended. At this stage Dave met Alan Bernstein and through the formation of Conservation Corporation the model was on its way to becoming a pan-African reality.

Opposite: Top, game drives start at dawn when the diurnal animals are most active and end after sunset when the nocturnal animals are waking up. Visitors are just about to discover an elephant even closer than the one they have been watching on their right, but the tracker, always observant, is watching carefully. Elephants are gentle creatures and will seldom get annoyed unless provoked.

Opposite: Below left, a tree squirrel scampers about and is quick to disappear into the canopy of a tree if alarmed. Below right, at the camps there is time to enjoy a book, a glass of wine and far more than a loaf of bread.

ON THE WINGS OF THE BATELEUR

It is written on the arched sky, it looks out from every star,
It is on the sailing cloud and in the invisible wind,
It is among the hills and valleys of the earth ....
It is the poetry of nature.
— *John Ruskin*

EPAIRING THE DAMAGED HABITAT under Ken Tinley's magic wand had been an incredibly heady and exciting experience for Dave and JV. It laid the foundation for one of the basic tenets of the Londolozi model: the experience and the knowledge gained at Londolozi could and should be exported to other areas of southern Africa and beyond, wherever it is needed.

By 1990 Dave had brought Londolozi to high professional standards while at the same time balancing the requirements of man against his responsibility to preserve the wilderness habitat. He believed he had a mission to use his knowledge to help counter the relentless inroads that man, for various reasons, was making on the scarce wilderness resources of the world. Unknown to him, six thousand miles away in London, Alan Bernstein saw Africa as an emerging market full of investment opportunity and with extensive dormant resources.

Alan had grown up in South Africa knowing all about Londolozi. His family were avid wildlife fans, his stepfather, Harry Gottlieb, was a great friend and business partner of Arthur Thomas who had married Helen Varty. Although he had been to Londolozi frequently in his youth, possibly because he was five years younger than Dave, they had not got to know each other well. In 1987 Alan had married and with his wife Sandy decided to spend a few years away from South Africa to assess their future. For a politically active person, South Africa presented a life of conflict, fear and uncertainty. A civil engineer by profession, he had found his real interest lay not in design and construction but in development. His first step in redirecting his career was to enroll at the renowned business school INSEAD in Fontainebleau where he completed an MBA. Here he met Jean-Claude Batault with whom he formed JHI International, a merchant banking operation based in London. Africa looked an area of immense opportunity to the two men. Communism was on the retreat. The conflict in Moçambique had ended. The war in Angola was unlikely to be sustained. The failure of African socialism was clear. Namibia was independent and the first prisoners from Robben Island had been released. Democracy in South Africa could not be far behind. For the first time in years there was hope.

With the help of Kevin Leo-Smith, managing director of a real estate company in Pietermaritzburg, Alan had identified what he believed to be a potential private game reserve near the Maputaland coast in KwaZulu/Natal. The land, steeped in Zulu history and culture, consisted in part of derelict sugar, cattle and pineapple farms. More significantly it formed a link between the Mkuzi Game Reserve and St. Lucia Game Reserve and was therefore of strategic importance to the ultimate development of a Greater St. Lucia Wetland Park.

Alan targeted Londolozi as an example of grassroots ecotourism development in southern Africa and arranged for JV to give a presentation on the

Above: Dave Varty and Alan Bernstein, founders of Conservation Corporation. Opposite: For over a century the natural systems of Maputaland were plundered of game and then butchered by poor farming. This saline coastal plain with its fig and fever forests and unique dry Sand forests should never have been farmed in the first place. This could not have been better illustrated than when farmers bulldozed mature fig and fever tree forests on the Mkuzi floodplain, planted bananas and then, the following season, claimed flood damage from the government. It was the only way they could make the land pay.

Above: An African fish eagle, *Haliaeetus vocifer*. Opposite: Phinda was exactly what Alan Bernstein and Dave were looking for; an extraordinarily beautiful land. To the east the vast open plain was fringed by the Indian ocean, to the west by the rugged Ubombo mountains. Within a relatively small area it held seven different ecosystems and a wonderful diversity of bird and animal life. Over millions of years the plain had periodically been inundated by the sea with the result that in general the land had only a thin layer of topsoil, all too easily destroyed by poor farming and specially by cattle and goats. African wildlife, with its ability to use the full spectrum of flora and its resistance to most diseases, was far better adapted to the land. It was ideal as an ecotourism destination, particularly with its wetland systems and lakes and, nearby, pristine beaches and sparkling sea.

A selection of Indian ocean seashells.

Londolozi model to a team of potential investors. Alan recalls the day the group arrived at Main Camp: "JV literally staggered onto the deck. He had malaria and was clearly out on his feet although he spoke valiantly for 45 minutes before asking Dave to take over."

The meeting transcended anything Dave or Alan could have imagined. "Alan brought a paradigm shift to conservation thinking," says Dave. "He spoke in terms of investment strategies, socio-economics and the utilisation of dormant assets." It was much further along the same road that they had started on 15 years earlier when they decided that ecotourism could make conservation a viable industry not reliant on donations or central government funding. Alan, thinking and reasoning, was effectively the left brain of a partnership; Dave, intuitive, holistic, imaginative, the right brain. Combined, they created a dynamic energy field. Both identified with the same objectives and philosophies.

Soon after their first meeting Dave wrote Alan a letter in which he set out his ideas for unlocking dormant assets in Africa through conservation tourism developments. "During our lifetime the southern African region will again open up and expertise such as we have could be put to enormous benefit," he wrote. His vision was of a conservation tourism development that would position itself in a partnership with people and nature. "If you can bring real funding to Africa," Dave told Alan, "I can show you how to wake up the wilderness."

While Kevin Leo-Smith worked on the incredibly delicate negotiating operation of securing options from the farmers, Alan and Dave started on a feasibility study and continued their search for the finance to buy an initial 14 000 hectares. Dave, who with John, had spent the early part of his Londolozi days ducking into the bush when their bank manager came looking for them, had had no exposure to international finance and was out of his depth with the numbers that Alan rolled off his tongue. But he learnt fast. They would need a minimum of R110 million to clean up and restock the land, put in fences, build at least two lodges and train local people up to Londolozi standards. Personally they could raise less than 5 percent of this figure. Alan decided they needed the umbrella of one of the big corporations in South Africa. As there was not going to be any short-term profit, they needed long-term funding and a sympathetic lender. They had the example of the Sabi Sand which earns R2000 a hectare per annum and has a land value many times that of the adjacent farmland to the west. In 1926 Charles Varty and Frank Unger paid £1236 for 4056 hectares, equivalent to 60 cents a hectare. By 1971 the value of the land had increased to R180 per hectare. Twenty-five years later the value had gone up to R8000 a hectare. Of even more significance, Sabi Sand land seldom changed hands and almost never came onto the open market. This is a trend that will increasingly be seen all over the world. The price of wilderness real estate will relate to its scarcity, not necessarily to its earning power.

Above: A flap-necked chameleon *Chamaeleo dilepis* which at night turns blue-white in colour.

Below: A black-backed jackal, as well as scavenging, will eat insects, birds' eggs, small mammals and fruit.

Opposite: An epauletted fruit bat, a warthog and baboons. Nature's bio-diversity, that is every single variation of life form from a single living cell to millions of insect, reptile, bird, fish and animal species, is a treasure chest of beauty that needs our protection.

Their first talks with Gencor, one of the 'big five' mining finance houses in South Africa, went extremely well. The Gencor board chaired by Derek Keyes was interested. That put Alan and Dave back to the drawing boards and when their report was ready, the board debated the issue. Alan remembers very clearly: "Around midday they gave us the thumbs up. The proposal was approved. We were euphoric. We didn't need a lift to get down the stairs. We literally floated on air." That night Dave and Shan, JV, Alan and Sandy celebrated. The next day they flew with the Gencor people to Richards Bay and drove with Kevin to the project area in KwaZulu/Natal. They had breakfast on the top of the Ubombo mountains, surveyed the vast plain below, looked at the rivers and wetlands, visited the pristine Maputaland coastline and flew back. Only then were they told that the next day as 'a formality' Gencor's holding company Sancorp, would have to ratify their decision. Still very excited, Dave and Alan went back in the morning to the same anteroom where two days earlier they had waited with trepidation the decision of the Gencor board. This time, totally unexpectedly, and for reasons unrelated to the ecotourism project, a different decision was handed out.

Alan says: "The bottom literally fell out of my world. I spent the weekend in the eastern Transvaal and walked what seemed like a 100 kilometres, wondering what to do next. Was this the end of our dream?" He came out of that weekend with a firm resolve that it was too good an idea to let go. For better or worse, somehow he was going to find the finance to launch their company which they had decided to name Conservation Corporation. He instructed Kevin to renew their options for a further three months.

The costs of renewing options, raising capital, preparing proposals and taking interested people to Maputaland kept on mounting but there were still no investors. The South African financial community for the most part was only prepared to lend where more than adequate security could be guaranteed. And although Nelson Mandela had been released sanctions were still in place and there was little chance of international funding. It was hands off South Africa. There was only one thing to do – go fishing.

Alan flew to Cape Town to meet Koos Jonker, the one person who understood their vision and could do something about it. Jonker, captain of the Western Province deep sea fishing team, was also chairman of Masterbond, a company which would go down as the largest financial collapse and subsequent fraud case in South Africa's history.

The deal drawn up with Masterbond was far from perfect. Instead of R110 million, they could only get R60 million and instead of long-term it was in short-term funding. But it was sufficient to get started. Conservation Corporation was launched and its first project which they called Phinda Resource Reserve was underway in KwaZulu/Natal. Phinda, the Zulu word for 'the return', described their goal: to put back the wildlife which had been virtually destroyed a century earlier. Londolozi's first logo had been a bateleur perched on a branch. With the launch of Conservation Corporation the bateleur was flying high. This was the symbol they adopted as their logo.

Dave and Alan now had a double load to carry. As well as getting started with development at Phinda and building the administrative and marketing infrastructure, there was an urgent need to replace Masterbond's short-term funding with long-term finance. A Hambros Bank team led by deputy chairman, Christopher Sporborg, and three dynamic, talented professional financiers all with strategic interests in South Africa, took up the challenge. Jan Newman and Jonathan Klein both had their roots in South Africa. Mark Getty was a member of one of the largest financial dynasties in the world. They went ahead and packaged a prospectus to sell bankrupt farms in northern Zululand to international investors.

A few months later Alan and Dave, armed with the prospectus, were on the 21st floor of the Ford Foundation trying to convince a group of American financiers why they should invest their money in a game reserve consisting of a cluster of bankrupt farms with no big game, in KwaZulu/Natal which appeared to be on the verge of civil war and in a country against which sanctions were still in place. And to cap it all, during the meeting a message was received that their South African bankers had gone bust! The portfolio manager who controlled billions of dollars, quite understandably, was more interested in lunch.

Despite these setbacks Hambros managed to keep the show on the road. Finance, urgently needed to repay Masterbond's curators, was being raised and Mark Getty, who played a pivotal role in launching Conservation Corporation, managed to interest his entire family in one single investment for the first time since the disposal of Getty Oil. He too believed that in the long term, investment on sound business principles in conservation in Africa had huge potential.

In the midst of all these negotiations, early in 1992 Dave received an interesting proposal. Would he and Alan discuss the future of the Ngala Game Reserve with Frans Stroebel of the S.A. National Parks Trust and Dr. Robbie Robinson, National Parks Board's chief executive? Hans Hoheisen whose family had owned the 14 000 hectare Ngala reserve adjoining the Kruger Park since 1938, had donated the property, valued at little short of R100 million, to the World Wide Fund for Nature. This was the largest single donation ever made to the WWF. The property was to be managed as an integral part of the Park. Robbie Robinson's view was that the Kruger National Park had no experience in running luxury game lodges for international travellers. His proposal was to engage a private operator to take over the hospitality side of the business, leaving the Kruger Park to look after the land and the wildlife. It was impossible to have a more fortuitous opportunity. A private sector/public sector partner-

ship gave Conservation Corporation a credibility rating far higher than its close association with Londolozi. When Dave signed the 10-year contract, Robbie Robinson asked Dave: "Is jy besig om bankrot te speel?" (Are you busy going bankrupt?) Dave's reply was that it was touch and go but if he signed the contract they would have a better chance of making it. Dave recalls: "Robbie picked up his pen, signed the paper, handed it to me and said: 'Good luck!'" For a government body, the decision to form a partnership with private enterprise was a complete break away from the past. "Dr. Robinson and Frans Stroebel made a visionary decision and created a model for future conservation tourism development in Africa," said Dave. "It has been enormously successful all round. We pay a rental for the use of the reserve and through a conservation committee participate actively with KNP officers in caring for the 14 000 hectare reserve. We are enormously indebted to Robinson and Stroebel for their courage."

Although Ngala was an answer to a prayer, giving them added stature as well as three legs on which to develop their marketing structure (Ngala, Phinda and Londolozi), they now had to find a further R4.5 million to develop Ngala.

Dave and Alan wasted no time in going back to their potential backers. Neale Axelson, financial director of AECI (African Explosives & Chemical Industries) and chairman of the company's pension fund, was the first to break ranks with South Africa's conservative business leaders. Axelson recognised the advantages which ecotourism could bring to rural Africa. Others followed: Anglo American, De Beers, Ernest Oppenheimer & Sons, Southern Life, Metropolitan Life, Federated Life. Within a short time Conservation Corporation had received sufficient funding from both local and international investors to repay their debt to Masterbond which they did, paying their debt early and in full.

Phinda was bought. The reserve was to make history as the biggest private wildlife development in southern Africa. And South Africa was immensely richer for it. But it was a long, hard road. When they took over the property, many areas were completely bankrupt through overuse of pesticides which had damaged the habitat and made it vulnerable to invasion by unproductive plant species while the wilderness was littered with broken power lines, derelict tractors, cattle grids and fences. In the entire area no more than 80 people earned an average per capita income of R450 per annum. Work started immediately on building dams and roads and restoring the natural wilderness applying Londolozi's land management principles: clearing the invasive acacia with bulldozers. Phinda Mountain Lodge was built on the hillside overlooking the great Maputaland coastal plain. The wildlife in the region at the beginning was limited to nyala, red duiker, a few rhino, wildebeest and an occasional suni, but after one of the biggest game restocking exercises ever undertaken in South Africa, Phinda's wildlife population took off. Within a few years herds of wildebeest and zebra, elephant and rhino were seen on the Mziki marsh. Nyala

Opposite: The Ngala Lodge, at the junction of the mopane forests and the Timbavati flood plain, was the first private lodge within the Kruger National Park. The lodge was rebuilt by Conservation Corporation in 1992.

Opposite below: Left, big prides of lion are frequently seen at Ngala – the Shangaan word meaning lion. Right, a giant eagle owl, *Bubo lacteus*. Dressed to kill, the giant eagle owl is a formidable predator including in its diet reptiles, frogs, fish, many birds and smaller mammals.

Above: A cheetah inspects chairs offloaded in preparation for one of the romatic bush dinners at Phinda. Sometimes these are set out under a giant *Acacia tortilis* 'umbrella thorn' tree and sometimes in a secluded clearing in the middle of one of the forests.

Grassroots development in the wilderness is an expensive business, even without having to buy the land and the massive restocking exercise. Going rates for white rhinos are R47 000, hippo R10 000 and giraffe R7000. Even a crested guineafowl costs R1000. Infrastructure is enormously expensive; access roads and runways have to be built, power and telephone links established sometimes over long distances, water supplies guaranteed even in dry seasons which means building dams. And one of the big cost items is staff training.

Right: Predators and their prey. Lion cubs will soon be old enough to make a meal of a suni lamb which is particularly vulnerable to leopards and pythons. A pygmy kingfisher, despite its name, lives off insects, frogs, lizards, crustaceans and spiders. A moon moth, *Argema mimosae*, belonging to the emperor moth family Saturniidae which includes the largest moths in the world.

Bateleur feathers.

Top: A suite at Phinda's lovely Forest Lodge built on the edge of a vlei in a unique dry Sand forest on the Maputaland coastal plain. Above: The living room at the Singita Lodge on the farm Ravenscourt in the Sabi Sand. Opposite: Flamingo on the Ngorongoro crater floor. Reticulated giraffe and zebra in East Africa.

Jewel beetle, *Chrysochroa lepida.*

and kudu could be sighted camouflaged in the acacia. Cheetah, leopard, hyena and lion stalked their prey. The bird life of Phinda had always been magnificent, particularly on the marshes and on the Mzinene river where fish eagles, herons, kingfishers, ducks, pygmy geese, gallinules and cormorants are some of the many birds to be found. With nature's bounty restored, Phinda has become a veritable paradise.

By 1993 the story of Phinda was only at its beginning. With just one lodge the property was simply not economically viable. Work started almost immediately on the beautiful Forest Lodge on the edge of the Sand forest in the northern sector of the reserve, increasing the total number of beds within the reserve to 72. Forest Lodge was completed at a cost of R7 million in November 1993. They opened their doors to international travellers – and no one came. As pre-election fever mounted, KwaZulu/Natal had become a battle zone.

Alan reasoned that there was only one solution: they needed to diversify geographically. Every country in Africa had experienced growing pains. Right then KwaZulu/Natal was experiencing bad days. Perhaps next year the focus could shift to another country in Africa. Hypothetically, if they spread themselves through ten different countries in Africa, there was a good chance they could have a 90 percent success rating all the time. Alan looked at the options available to them and targeted the one person who he felt could not only open new markets for them but could also directly help with their expansion into other countries. Geoffrey Kent of Abercrombie & Kent fame is regarded as the doyen of the safari business. As well as having a huge marketing operation, Kent owned a number of lodges in Kenya and Tanzania. Alan had heard that Kent could be interested in selling his East African properties.

Once he had tracked down Geoff Kent in Florida, Alan called Dave away from a skiing holiday with his family and two days later they met Kent in the United States. Alan proposed that Kent should sell Conservation Corporation his ground operations which included Kichwa Tembo in Kenya's Masai Mara and the fabulous site of a somewhat down-at-heel Ngorongoro Crater Lodge. They would also have the opportunity to join up with an experienced and talented management team which was of critical importance to their expansion into East Africa. Occupancy rates in Kenya averaged well over 80 percent which meant an immediate improvement in turnover. Tanzania was seen as the next great African destination and, at last, there were signs that South Africa's long isolation was ending. Most important of all an association with Kent would give them an immediate entry into international markets through the Abercrombie & Kent worldwide network.

"We then went back to our shareholders and put our cards on the table," said Dave. "They were superb. We got their full support and after 18 months of tough negotiation we expanded into East Africa. Kenya's tourism industry in particular was very mature and the deep experience through all levels of staff provided the opportunity for stimulating cross flows of talents and cultures."

There remained one anomaly. With Conservation Corporation growing by leaps and bounds, Dave as chairman of the young company and co-owner of Londolozi found his interests divided. Conservation Corporation had taken over marketing Londolozi and Dave sometimes had to sit on both sides of the table, negotiating agreements between the two companies. The solution was for Londolozi to be brought under the same umbrella. In 1994 the Vartys and Allan Taylor signed a 10-year management contract with Conservation Corporation.

The knowledge that Dave and John had acquired during their 20 years of developing Londolozi, Ken Tinley's acute observations and Shan's understanding of people and the vital importance of the human resource factor had provided the 'oxygen' for the development of Conservation Corporation. Londolozi was also a pool of talented and experienced people from which Conservation Corporation could draw. Many people to whom home meant 'Londolozi' found themselves elsewhere: travelling to Phinda or to Ngala or to East Africa imparting the Londolozi way. It was a trend that would continue. Some people thrived on the greater opportunity for an exciting career path. Others did not.

Conservation Corporation now had two well established operations; Londolozi and Kichwa Tembo. Alan Bernstein says: "There was no doubt that this helped enormously with getting our developing operations into the market." Soon after that Luke Bailes, owner of the lovely Singita Private Game Reserve in the Sabi Sand and a close friend of the Vartys, gave them a huge vote of confidence, placing Singita in the Conservation Corporation stable. Luke has worked for 15 years rehabilitating the land at Singita which is another example of what can be achieved with time and effort.

At the time of the East African negotiations, Geoff Kent had been working on a tourism development opportunity in Zimbabwe. As part of Conservation Corporation's deal he introduced Dave and Alan to Lovemore Chihota, a successful and influential Zimbabwean businessman. "He had a magnificent concession," said Dave. "Fifty thousand hectares of unbelievable wilderness west of the Victoria Falls including 15 kilometres of Zambezi river frontage – and he wanted a manager." Alan on the other hand was adamant. In keeping with their original vision, Alan wanted a partnership. He was not prepared to build up a name, make it into a wonderful tourist destination only to be kicked out when the profits started to roll in. It seemed to be a total impasse with no way around. The Zimbabweans expressed their nervousness of expatriates known for stripping wealth out of the country, but Chihota did need expertise. This was the opening Dave had been looking for. "We're not expatriates from another continent," he said. "We have no other country except Africa. We were born here and so were our grandfathers. We regard ourselves as Africans and

Above: A vulturine guineafowl.

Opposite: The Victoria Falls. Below left, a Masai bride in traditional regalia. Centre, a spectacular Makishi dancer of the Lozi people who inhabit the upper reaches of the Zambezi river. Right, Thomson's gazelles found in their thousands on the East African plains.

Flame lily, *Gloriosa superba*.

we have committed our business to creating wealth and working with the rural people of Africa." The tone of the meeting changed and the eventual outcome was a partnership between the South African company and the Zimbabwean government. In August 1996 the Matetsi Game Reserve owned by Conservation Corporation Zimbabwe opened. Lovemore Chihota became the Zimbabwean company's first chairman.

Conservation Corporation was growing and the timing could not have been more perfect. South Africa was just starting to be seen as a new source of strength for the whole of sub-Saharan Africa. Tourism had come back to life. In the first two years after the miracle of the 1994 elections, the number of tourists had increased at an annualised 17 percent, without doubt helped by the rugby World Cup in 1995 and the tremendous interest in South Africa's cricket, soccer and golfing stars. But South Africa was only getting 0.7 percent of the world's travellers. "If we could shift that up to two percent," Dave says, "it would make an enormous difference to rural Africa.

"We also believe that our ideal development plan is through partnerships. In South Africa our partners are the Kruger National Park and the KwaZulu/Natal Parks Board, in Zimbabwe it is the government. In Kenya the owners of the land are the Masai; in Tanzania Tanapa and Ngorongoro Crater Authority own the land. We are therefore all partners." In retrospect Dave considers that buying Phinda was inappropriate. "It tied up millions of rands and put a huge burden on us when we should have been concentrating on developing conservation tourism and creating wealth in rural areas. Even now with Phinda running at 80 percent occupancy rates, we have still not achieved the return on investment that would demonstrate our complete success to our shareholders. In the future if the government makes undeveloped land available to private enterprise, it will help enormously with rural economies and with the development of our unique tourism industry. We are negotiating for the Phinda land to be handed back to the conservation authorities which ultimately, I believe, will be the breakthrough to the full realisation of the natural wealth of the St. Lucia and Maputaland region."

Fortunately at Phinda it is possible to put more development on the land than in the Sabi Sand. Because of its location within the framework of the future Greater St. Lucia Wetland Park, Phinda's visitors have options to any number of outdoor activities; birdwatching from hides, game drives, a mini-Okavango cruise on the Mzinene river, visiting neighbouring fig and fever forests where Pels fishing owls nest and where you can track black rhino, deep sea fishing on the world's southernmost coral reefs or swimming and snorkelling off the pristine Maputaland beaches. The result is that they have the capacity to absorb a third lodge into the reserve without taking away the exclusivity that makes Conservation Corporation's destinations such a special experience.

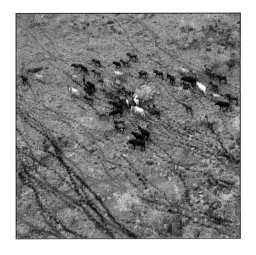

"Our core philosophy at Conservation Corporation is, and always will be, sustainability," says Dave. "Without the basic requirements taught us by Ken Tinley – care of land, care of wildlife and care of people; guests, staff and the communities adjacent to our operations, we would have no hope of sustaining our wildlife and achieving long-term economic success. In particular we cannot hope in Africa to maintain exclusive wildlife areas if rural people on the other side of our boundaries live in a wasteland of donga erosion and silted rivers, have no opportunity for employment, and in all probability have a rising crime rate and a serious aids problem. Our role is to make a really meaningful contribution to these communities by raising living standards through education and training and giving people the opportunity to be proud of their achievements."

There are many ways in which conservation benefits can go beyond the barrier of a fence. The Kwa-Mduku community which neighbours Phinda was the first to benefit from the founding by Conservation Corporation of the Rural Investment Fund. A R650 000 clinic was built to serve the community of 8000 people. Six schools were provided with new classrooms, a community centre was built, while many people have been assisted in developing their own small business operations. One success story, again based on Londolozi experience, is a charcoal industry, using wood from Phinda's bush-clearing operations, which now markets its charcoal in Europe and the Middle East.

Adjoining Londolozi, two farms, Huntington and Justicia, owned by the tribal community, have an exciting future. The land is not good for farming and many of those who have tried using the land for cattle grazing have lost money. One local man lost 180 head of cattle – his entire fortune – in the last drought. The Development Bank of Southern Africa has listed the Huntington community of 4500 people amongst the poorest settlements in the country with 40 percent unemployment and an average wage of R350 a month earned by those lucky enough to find a job. Solly Mohaule, Conservation Corporation's rural development officer and Allan Taylor, Londolozi co-owner and Conservation Corporation shareholder, are discussing a joint venture development of 2000 hectares on the western boundary of the Sabi Sand with the local leaders. But the road back from apartheid and the homeland system is fraught with problems. The old tribal system has broken down but has not yet been replaced by an effective management structure within the community. They do not hold title deeds and there is uncertainty of land tenure. There is also an understandable lack of trust of white people. Despite all these difficulties, Allan is working steadily on the project which includes the construction of an airport to meet the requirements of the entire Sabi Sand and the start of the community's own game reserve. With Allan helping them there is every chance that they will succeed.

The steep growth of Conservation Corporation put enormous pressure on its human resources. Dave and Alan Bernstein decided it was time they brought

Top: Much of southern Africa is totally unsuitable for cattle ranching. All too frequently when one dry season follows another, the grass disappears and cattle die of disease or starvation.

Above: Traditional industries such as weaving from rushes and reeds, which for centuries have been harvested on a sustainable basis, have almost ceased to exist because modern methods of harvesting have destroyed the plant beds.

Opposite: Never a dull moment at Phinda, Africa's only game reserve that includes dolphins, whale sharks and sea turtles.

Above: There are many places in Africa which seem as inhospitable and barren as a lunar landscape. Yet some animals have adapted to the harsh conditions and have learnt to survive, licking dew from leaves before the moisture vanishes under the rays of the hot sun, digging for roots, or finding a waterhole or an underground spring. In the vast desert an oryx and a cheetah, pass one another without an upward glance. A squirrel makes the most of a ripe melon which will supply sufficient moisture for its survival.

Opposite: A desert black rhino, one of the world's most threatened species, thrives in the incredibly beautiful habitat of the Tswalu Private Desert Reserve in the north-west Cape.

in a professional manager to administer the business. Their first choice was Steve Fitzgerald who had advised the Varty's in the early days when they were building up the Londolozi model. Steve and his wife Nicky needed little persuasion. It was going to be exciting and a great challenge for them both. Under Steve's management, Conservation Corporation has soared. Today it employs over 2000 people with roughly 20 000 dependants and has more than 24 different destinations in many countries south of the Sahara. Most exciting of all, the group's reputation has spread and people with potential projects continually knock on its door. The result has been that there is enormous opportunity for staff to learn and to follow career paths in ecotourism. To help staff attain service excellence, a training school has been built at Phinda to which people from all over Africa are being drawn.

The year 1995 marked the emergence of a new type of investor into conservation. Many individuals with wealth at their disposal to live out their dreams committed their money and talents to restoring the fragile ecological linkages which make up this great planet. Stephen Boler's 75 000 hectare Tswalu Private Desert Reserve in the north-west Cape is a refuge for desert black rhino and elephant. Makalali is the dream of Charles Smith and his late brother Joe, to build a reserve linking the Drakensberg mountains to the eastern seaboard. Lovemore Chihota has influenced his government to convert a hunting concession into a photographic safari destination and stimulate tourism in Zimbabwe. These people have seen the huge advantage of aligning themselves with Conservation Corporation.

Alan believes that in the long term they will need to obtain a listing so as to attract international and national professional equity funding and diversify Conservation Corporation's shareholder base. "In August 1995 we planned to launch 'Africa Resources' on the London Alternative Investment Market," says Alan, "but at the eleventh hour we decided to call it off. We would have been the third company listed on this market. We then regrouped with Hambros and our shareholders who, in the rapidly improving South African market, agreed to delay the listing and to support the company fully in its expansion plans.

"A year later, in August 1996, South African Breweries, through its wholly-owned subsidiary Southern Sun, became a major shareholder in Conservation Corporation. Half of the R30 million agreement was used to offset the purchase from Southern Sun of Bongani Mountain Lodge and Zululand Tree Lodge, two lodges, bordering state-owned parks. These properties fitted into our business far more comfortably than they did in the big hotel operations of Southern Sun. In addition we went ahead with the private placement of US$15 million specifically to acquire properties in Tanzania which would create superb guest itineraries complementing the redeveloped Ngorongoro Crater Lodge. These properties included the Grumeti River Camp and Kleins Camp in the Serengeti,

Maji Moto Camp in Lake Manyara National Park and Mnemba Island Club off the coast of Zanzibar.

Alan considers that Conservation Corporation is entering a new phase. He has discovered that the key to success is quality and style of service and the wilderness experience. "We have a marvellous team of people at our camps in the high spots of the African continent. It's the people and the wildlife that bring our guests back again and again," he says. "We started out close to the Maputaland coast, we've expanded into incredibly beautiful areas in Africa. Perhaps we may take our philosophy further, into the forests of South America or beyond. It could be that we will spread our story across the globe and maybe there will one day be Conservation Corporations on every continent. Our prime goal will be to ensure that our philosophy is carried through; care of the land, the wildlife, the communities and of our guests."

Dave gets phone calls from all over the world. "They have one common theme," he says. "People who have achieved great success in business and made fortunes now wish to put something back into the natural world by buying real estate and restoring its natural beauty." Dave hopes the concept that began at Londolozi will spread: "Right now a team from Ecuador is visiting us to look at our 'model' and we are discussing a project in the Pantanal, a massive wetland in the heart of Brazil similar to the Okavango and with a bird life that is fantastic. Other possibilities exist in the marginal low-rainfall areas of Australia and in Indonesia where safe havens for tiger, Indian elephant, honey bear and Sumatran rhino are urgently needed in the face of the devastation taking place in the region. One of the most exciting ideas to emerge is the transfrontier park concept, linking vast tracts of land regardless of national boundaries under multi-use wildlife schemes, making Africa the greatest wildlife theatre on earth."

Perhaps at the dawning of the Aquarian age, when the impact of man's damage to the earth is so visible and our understanding of the intricacies of the working of the planet's systems has sufficiently advanced, people will be prepared to lead the charge towards the restoration of the planet's precious and valuable resources. Conservation Corporation is one small cog in the gigantic wheel that could make a difference. But it needs to show that it can be successful in all three aspects of its operations: ecologically, socially and financially. First and foremost the rules of the game require financial success. Conservation Corporation is rapidly moving towards achieving this goal.

Christopher Sporborg, deputy chairman of Hambros, London, is non-executive chairman of Conservation Corporation's main board which consists of an international group of shareholders. Other members of the board include Judge Bill Newsom, Tom Woodhouse and Mark Getty who represent Getty family interests, Jonathan Klein who had left Hambros with Mark Getty to develop Getty Communications, Terence Woolley representing the AECI Pension Fund and Ron Stringfellow Southern Sun's managing director. Dave, Alan Bernstein and Steve Fitzgerald represent the core executive management team.

Opposite: From top left clockwise, Makalali, a linkage between the Drakensberg mountains and the Kruger National Park; Matetsi on the Zambezi river 40 kilometres upstream from the Victoria Falls; Kitchwa Temba in Kenya's Masai Mara and Mnemba Island off Zanzibar.

THE END IS THE BEGINNING

The wildlife of today is not ours to dispose of as we please,
we have it in trust, we must account for it to those who come after.
— *King George V*

 N AFRICA THE RENEWER OF LIFE is not the sun – although some may tell you otherwise. The sun bares the earth and bakes it as hard as concrete. Then wind erosion starts to wear away the surface, particle by particle, layer by layer, until the sand starts to pile up and move in the great waves of a Sahara or Kalahari desert. Life on the African continent, as everywhere, is sustained by the protective mantle of the atmosphere. Within that atmosphere water vapour collects until huge cumulus storm clouds form spiralling 20 kilometres towards the heavens. Suddenly the clouds release their load and rain, the renewer of life, comes tumbling towards the earth. On the Zambezi valley escarpment 600 millimetres of rain have been recorded between sunset and sunrise. In the Great Rift Valley of Kenya, 120 millimetres of rain have fallen in 30 minutes. In South Africa great cloudbursts periodically thunder from the skies. And then comes a time of drought. No clouds, no rain. Day after day the relentless heat and dust. This is Africa. A paradox, a savage land, a sensitive land. A fragile land.

What shield has Africa got from a slow withering death? There is another mantle protecting the earth; grass which first appeared 60 million years ago. The combination of thousands of different plants with their slender green blades has created the greatest pastures on earth. If there is grass cover, every drop of rain will hit a blade of grass and then run gently down into the soil. Instead of the rainwater rushing away, the soil's moisture content increases. The water-table, the most remarkable of all water storage systems, rises and the earth is prepared to survive another long period without rain. Nature, so much smarter than man, has built its dams out of sight of the sun. The grass will grow covering and protecting the earth. Wild animals will graze and move on leaving their droppings, increasing the nitrogen in the soil. Dave calls this nature's virtuous cycle.

Then comes man imposing his demands on the land, building roads and homes, bringing in cattle and stripping the earth of its grass cover to plant crops. Along comes the rain. Now each drop of rain hits a bared patch of baked earth. Instead of soaking into the earth, it bounces. And as it bounces it gathers a few particles of soil. Then it starts to move, gaining momentum and gathering an ever increasing load of silt. It reaches a stream, the stream joins a river and becomes a mighty angry brown torrent racing out of control, removing river banks, trees, animals and even taking dams out in its relentless rush towards the sea where it offloads silt and damages marine ecology.

Once this vicious cycle is underway the next step that man takes has been referred to by Bill Mollison as 'plundering a failing wilderness'. Water is continually pumped from the rivers and boreholes are sunk for irrigation and to support a growing urban population. And so the water-table falls. The rivers become weaker. Eventually they stop flowing in dry seasons. This is the beginning of the

Above: Three of the most important elements on our planet; rain clouds, grass which protects the topsoil, and dung which adds nutrients to the soil and helps to germinate seeds eaten by animals and birds. Fungi, which inhabit an elephant's stomach, are deposited in its dung.

Opposite: A leopard's beautiful spotted coat provides insulation against the cold and protection when it rains.

Above: Bronwyn and Boyd Varty represent the next generation who will care for Londolozi. For them and for Savannah, just as it was for Dave and JV, Londolozi is a place to learn about nature, its inexhaustible bounty and about the value of all life.

Catopsilia florella, African migrant.

end. Eventually a beautiful wilderness will be transformed into a desert. This is what is happening in the bushveld where the Kruger National Park and most of South Africa's private game reserves are situated.

In Mpumalanga the rivers – particularly the Sabie, Sand, Olifants, Timbavati, Letaba, Komati and Crocodile – which flow from the Drakensberg escarpment eastwards to the Indian ocean, have huge demands made on them. In the high catchment areas where these rivers start, the frequent burning of grasslands to provide grazing for sheep has led to massive erosion and silting of rivers. Further downstream pine and eucalypt forests covering thousands of hectares both on the hillsides and in the valleys have destroyed sponge areas and draw vast quantities of water from the soil. In the lowveld avocado, citrus, mango, banana, macadamia and pecan nut plantations are irrigated by water pumped from the rivers during the low-flow winter months. In the bushveld where large communities sprang up in the 70s, cattle and goats finally have their turn in damaging river banks and taking off water. Along the way the riverine habitat has been invaded by many exotic species ranging from American bramble and Mauritius thorn introduced to South Africa to use for cattle kraals and bomas, to jacaranda, syringa, wattle, eucalypt and pine, their seeds spread by birds and wind. This army of exotic species clogs the rivers and reduces flows.

The drought which ended in December 1995 devastated farmlands and game reserves alike. Many farmers were bankrupted; cattle died of starvation, crops failed. The cost of fire control of the exotic plantations ran into millions. Game reserves were forced to cull drastically to ensure that a nucleus of each species survived. Then the rains came. Dam walls were breached. Rivers tore down bridges in their fury. Millions of tons of topsoil found their way into the Indian ocean. The next drought could be worse. There is one certainty; following Africa's pattern of feast or famine, it will not be too long in coming.

The greater natural system from the mountains to the coastline needs to be managed ecologically ignoring man-made fences, boundaries and borders. Such a step would entail a revolution in government and provincial authorities' planning, but it is not beyond the realms of possibility. The relentless drying-out process, sometimes deceptively masked by a season of good rains, must be recognised and counter-measures taken if the 21st century is to hold any promise for future generations in southern Africa.

When Dave and John followed Ken Tinley's instructions, they were reinstating nature's virtuous cycle by ensuring the rain that fell on their land did not run down roads or eroded gulleys and dongas. It soaked into the earth and the grasses flourished. It did not matter whether there was slow gentle rain or a cloudburst. A thick mantle of grass would cope. Dave and John are passionate about Africa's wilderness habitats. In 1993, when the new Zoeknog dam in Lebowa collapsed, the flooded Sand river carried millions of tons of topsoil downstream. Dave went on prime time TV news to attack the government responsible for the mismanagement of the river. "Our river has been strangled and is dying," he roared. "I used to swim there as a child – what are we doing to our children's heritage?" It was not just the Sand river Dave was referring to. The wilderness heritage of Africa is unique. The people of Africa should be its custodians, not its destroyers. "We learnt a lesson from nature," says Dave, "and one we must never forget. If you want to have a self-sustaining operation in the wilderness you must invest in the land before you take anything out."

Big business is only part of the problem but it could be the leading force in the solution. "Change won't come by making laws to redirect the big corporations," says John. "It will come from within as more and more younger people, aware and in tune with the drama of the conflict between man and the planet, take the lead. Some of the big corporations led by a new generation of thinkers, are starting to clean up the rivers, but it is a huge and costly job and everyone, the industrialists, the farmers and the communities, need to be involved. In the long run all will benefit because the water-table on their lands, which has visibly fallen during the past 30 years, will rise again. The big corporations have the resources to clean up the atmosphere, the oceans, the rivers and wetlands and to care for our remaining wilderness habitats. I believe that soon corporate decisions will not be taken only on the basis of what is good for the bottom line, but whether it will enhance the longer term balance sheet of the environment, the communities, the country and the planet.

"Fortunately homo sapiens is an amazingly creative and intelligent animal. Provided there are sufficient people in power who care, there is yet a chance to create a greater harmony and balance in the world and to direct the future away from one in which mankind, through overpopulation and destruction of the environment, will be put at the mercy of natural systems; fire, flood, famine, drought and disease."

* * * * *

Seventy years have passed since Charles Varty and Frank Unger first set foot on Sparta and pitched their tents on the banks of the Sand river. They met up with communities whose forebears had for many generations been hunter/gatherers. They had lived in harmony with nature with a deep respect for animals and an intuitive ability to understand them. These were the people who at the beginning of this century were outlawed as poachers, a word associated with the vicious destruction of species for short-term gain. The real damage to the wildlife in the last century came not from the hunter/gatherers but from traders in ivory and skins, from development and from flawed political ideology.

All over South Africa concerned people are working towards securing more and more land as wildlife conservancies and protecting natural habitats.

Top: Lightning strikes the bushveld. Above: JV, once nicknamed 'Tilu' (lightning) says: "Whether this fragile planet can support a population of 10 billion people is theoretical stuff for statisticians. I believe that if we are to survive, we must learn to live in harmony with everything that lives and brings life. The alternative will be massive poverty, the rich getting richer, the poor getting poorer, the rip and strip, escalation of crime, the breakdown of spiritual values, the family unit and everything that is good in our lives."

Left column: Both predators and prey come in many shapes and sizes and are superbly adapted to attack or defend themselves. A colourful praying mantid, its two bulging compound eyes and three simple eyes enable it to be an extremely efficient hunter. A wingless female toad grasshopper is so well camouflaged that among dead leaves or on the branch of a tree, it completely disappears until it moves. A tinker reed frog, *Hyperolius tuberilinguis*, can leap to safety out of the path of a fish or a bird while a Nile crocodile is forced out of its usual lethargy by the strong current of the flooding Sand river.

Right column: A whitefronted bee-eater, *Merops bullockoides*, is able to take flying insects on the wing. Its long burrows which it digs into river banks for nestlings also provide a place of safety from fierce summer storms or from birds of prey. A blue waxbill, *Uraeginthus angolensis*, almost defenceless against raptors except for its quick flight, ensures the survival of its species by living in flocks of up to 40 birds. An immature bateleur, *Terathopius ecaudatus*, and a male coqui francolin, *Francolinus coqui*, which derives its name from its call repeated over and over, 'coqui, coqui, coqui'.

Opposite: Cheetah are only capable of relatively short bursts of speed and are at their most vulnerable to hyena and other larger predators after a kill. Impala virtually fly through the air when alarmed.

Eggs of the African Jacana.

Above: Elephants are creatures with memories and timetables and they will return to the same place, perhaps several seasons hence, looking for the same ripening fruit, lush grasses and waterhole. Their ability to recall and their wisdom are perhaps beyond our comprehension.

Blossoms of a *Combretum zeyheri*, the large fruited bushwillow. This tree is easily recognised by the clusters of large four-winged seeds which change in colour from green to pale yellow-brown in autumn.

The movement of private people entering this domain and taking over what was previously almost exclusively the responsibility of government, has escalated in recent years and forms a powerful base for Africa's growing ecotourism industry. Many corporations are backing this endeavour.

In the two decades since JV, Dave and Shan began their R3-a-day Londolozi wilderness trails there has been a revolution in man's interaction with, and attitudes towards, wildlife. The Varty's saw the need to care for wildlife but were confronted by two conflicting views; the emotionally-charged wilderness movement and Ken Tinley's 'if it pays it stays' highly pragmatic view. "Neither was perfect," says John. "We saw the untold benefits of Tinley's proposals and at the same time we understood the wilderness movement. Midway between was ecotourism. It was the compromise we took. Ecotourism gave us the money to repair the land, care for the wildlife and to provide opportunity for a sustainable economic substructure for rural communities. It is however a double-edged sword. The impact of ecotourism needs to be finely balanced against the integrity of the wilderness. It is not an easy task."

There are many advantages in Tinley's sustainable utilisation programme, that is, 'pruning' nature by only taking a few animals or birds in a planned and scientific way and ensuring the continued productivity of the species. Conservationist hunters still provide one of the best ways of raising funds for care of habitats and protection of species. Some people agree. Others do not. Many questions need to be answered. As a conservationist one asks is it ethical to hunt a 15-year-old lion for a fee of $30 000, a portion of which would be used for conservation? Or should the lion be left to a 'natural' death within a year when he is too old to fend for himself?

Perhaps the world is caught in a philosophy that is only now gaining momentum. Is modern man, with all his intelligence, still part of nature's cycle? Or has he evolved into a new role? Is it possible for man to live in harmony with all life on the planet and see himself as part of the whole intricate web of nature, understanding the vision of man and animal co-existing? Could we ever hope to recreate a Garden of Eden? Perhaps it is too much to ask that man, who cannot live together peacefully with his own kind, should be expected to live in harmony with all other species.

John compares people's awareness today to what it was at the start of the century: "People went in fear of wildlife," he says. "They had guns to protect themselves and they killed if they as much as saw a lion. Our awareness that all animals have feelings, emotions and a culture of their own has journeyed a long way since then. The few people who came in contact with Shingalana found it one of the most memorable and thrilling experiences of their lives.

"I have met people who are working on communication with dolphins and whales. I have put my hand on the head of an elephant and felt the vibration

Above: A whitewinged widow bird *Euplectes albonotatus.*

Left: In 1898 when President Kruger proclaimed the Sabie Game Reserve there were no elephants. They had fled from the sounds of gunfire into the almost impenetrable forests of Moçambique. When the guns were silenced, the elephants returned to the west where they remembered there was ideal country in which to roam. By 1926, when the Kruger Park was proclaimed and Charles Varty set up his first camp on the Sand river, there was only a single herd of about 25 animals to the north of the Olifants river. As they increased in numbers an arbitrary decision was taken by the Park's authorities to limit the elephant population to 7500. And so for the next 38 years elephants were culled. That was until 1996 when Dr. Robbie Robinson – head of the KNP – questioned the basis of this decision and put elephant culling on hold. And so the elephants of the eastern Transvaal, once almost destroyed, have turned a full circle since the arrival of man.

of its communication mechanism. I've lived with a lion and leopards, played with tigers. My own personal experiences have taught me that there are wild animals with more equitable characters than many humans – and *vice versa*. Science has shown us that animals do communicate. In another few years perhaps we will be able to understand what they are saying." Wherever John has travelled he has found a greater understanding and reverence for wild animals. "This global consciousness is only just gathering momentum and could totally change our attitudes and our scientific management of wildlife habitats."

For many people, not only Nelson Mandela, Londolozi is a haven where all nature is in rhythm and in harmony. Visitors feel a balance slowly returning to their lives even after a few days in this magical wilderness alongside the Sand river. There is always time to reflect inwardly as well as to observe the natural beauty of the surroundings: a soft spring leaf uncurls, a lovely butterfly settles on a flower, a golden spiderweb shines in the last rays of the sun, the birth of a young impala emphasises the cycle of life.

Perhaps it is this unsophisticated beauty that helps us distinguish between the real and the ephemeral in our lives. The space helps us gain a better perspective on problems that too often cloud our vision. Or perhaps it is the very vulnerability of wildlife that reminds us of our own fragile humanity and the precious and finite moments of our own lives. Whatever it is, emotional problems disappear, tension fades and even health improves. Being close to nature can heal the mind, the body and the soul. There is not one religion that does not teach a renewal of faith, of mental strength and of physical well-being by escaping from the strains of life to be at peace with nature.

The story of Londolozi, of reinstating nature's virtuous cycle, has no end because it sets its sights on infinity. A time beyond our lives and the lives of our children. It grew out of a love for the wild and a desire to leave at least some parts of Africa as they have been since the beginning of time; where the wide panorama at dawn and at dusk is all the proof we need of the existence of God.

It is a story that continues at Londolozi.

ROLL OF HONOUR

Lynn Ascham, Sherry King, Moz Wolhuter, Howard Mackie, Joe Venter, Struan Murless, Tony Lee, Craig Troeberg, Dave Lawrence, Gavin & Marilyn Joyce, Dale McKnight, Mike Myers, Janine Ovendale, Melanie Dolton-Brown, Ve Mascall, Marita Wentzel, Map Ives, Heather & Tony Hull, Liz Westby-Nunn, Elmon Mhlongo, Spook Sithole, Margo Roodt, Candy Meagher, Sherreen McLintock, Ian & Moira Thomas, Andre Goosen, Tedd Schorman, Lex Hes, Josh Whyte, Dave Wright, Pete Anderson, Ken & Lynn Maggs, Paddy Hagelthorn, Pete Le Roux, Pete Pyburn, Philip Knight, Elsje Lagaay, Mike & Pippa Beaumont, Gill Routledge, Lana van der Walt, Mike Penman, Jetje Lagaay, Jane Halstead, Chris Badger, Clive Jones, Guy Arkel, Jacqui Hill, Mike Barge, Pete & Penny Arnot, Hugh Marshall, Waynne McLintock, Warren Samuels, Heather McCullough, Lynn Melle, Marion Olie, Darren Saunders, Keith Schaper, Natalie Kitto, Carol Mommsen, Leigh Watson, Trish Tippett, Lillian Diender, BJ Watson, Allan Taylor, Tony & Dee Adams, Julie Holl, Clare McDonald, Andrew Paterson, Gaynor Watt, Barbara Bekker, Dave & Cath Kane- Berman, Ian & Sheila Hepburn, Chick Roche, Pat Donaldson, Sheena Boardman, Andy Anderson, James Marshall, Trevor Lindegger, Pete & Yvonne Short, Ronnie McKelvey, Rob Ketchington, Alistair Rankin, Richard de la Rey, Anne Sweetman, Kim Hebden, Gail Aronson, Iain de Beer, Paul Allen, Mel Piëst, Liz Farren, Jane Twycross, Bruce Simpson, Dumi Mpanza, Richard Siwele, Richard Mhlongo, Chris Irwin, Penny Main, Robyn Lawler, Justin Earle, Graham Vercueil, Andrew Lewis, Gary Lotter, Mark Tennant, Sandros Sihlangu, Chris Kane-Berman, Debbie Lowe, Solly Mohaule, Siphiwe Ubisi, Ian & Samantha Johnson, Ina Sonnenmoser, Ian Boyd, Michele Postma, Jacqui Evans, Nicky Paterson, Kerry Parker, Stella Brandsma, Lew Rood, Jane Conyngham, Mike Norris, Dave Bunyard, Tish Stewart, Monica Besner, Maureen Tobitt, Howard Geach, Mandy Chambers, Lameck Sibanda, Ray & Lesley Boyder, Mairead Schaper, Linda Arthur, Alan Bernstein, Anne Lee, Natalie Abratt, Marisa Laubscher, Vinolia Monamo, Neil & Nadine Clark, Mark McJanet, Anton Nel, Maureen Watson, Brian Watson, Standish O'Grady, Ethne Cameron, Ian & Merle Whyte, Michelle Thermann-Seago, Natalie Bagatta, Petra Borner, Garth Johnson, Nicole Young, Steuart Pennington, Suzanne Vine, Tessa Redman, Nicky Schoeman, Bert van der Linde, Margaret Kinsman, Marianne Kingsburgh, Linda Duff, Janet Rundel, Adré Venter, Bobby & Millie Lawrence, Saul & Wendy Braun, Neil & Susie Scott, Mike Davies, Andy & Di Marthinussen, Herbert Kahn, Peter & Mary Campbell, Ian Simms, Peter & Denise McFall, Pat Craig, Gert & Els Verf, Ken & Val Humphries, Dave & Miriam Meltzer, Richard Hawkins, Anthea McGregor, Neil & Morag Hulett, James Fitzgerald, Derrick & Jenny Hamlyn, Ross & Renee Parry-Davies, Steve & Nicky Fitzgerald, Ginger Gray, Lyn Eayrs, Paul & Alison Bannister, Dennis & Jenny Jooste, Gerry & Jill Brown, Richard Willis, Lorette Taylor, Alison Muldoon, Katheryn Tully, Eric & Liz Delmont, Rupert & Barbara Jeffries, Kobus & Valma Botha, Liz McGrath, Rupert Lorimer, Beth de Wet, Rob Clark, Stan Nel, Clive & Wendy Lucas-Bull, Bryan West, Aynne Vinnicombe, Andre de Beer, William Masenya, Windy Setshedi, Ashley Harris, Sheila Steenkamp, Lara Kriegsch, Kathryn Terry, Mike & Sue Wassung, Linda Figueria, Ken Hermer, Kerry Ochse, Sonja Hladik, Tonya Siebert, Natalie Jooste, Byron Ross, Pieter Siebert, Alex van den Heever, Reg Taylor, John Mohaud, Stuart Levine, Richard & Gail Hancock, Ruth Molefi, Lesley Simpson, Enos Mabuza, Di Riddell, Tony Stubbs, Rose Ramsey, Barry & Val Sinclair, Rufos Voorspuy, Winky & Wendy Ringo,

SPONSORING SUBSCRIBERS

Steve Bales
Gallien Global Vision, Incorporated
Mary Susan Gallien-Clinton & J.D. Clinton
Peter Gallo
Hazel de Quervain
Julia & Joseph Gould
Londolozi Productions
Douglas & Pippa Hutchison
Hannelore & Otto Richter
Ms Pierrette Schlettwein
Maidie Varty
Margi Taylor & Lorry Phillips of Margi Taylor & Associates
Alex & Anne Marie van Heeren

COLLECTORS' EDITION

BJ Watson
Eric Buchanan
Don Barrell & family
Danie Ferreira
Barry & Di Beningfield
Peter & Yvonne Short & family
Sidney L. Frankel
Michael M. Katz
Suthep Musicharal
Andrew, Anthea & Matthew McGregor
Intu Afrika Kalahari Game Reserve
Howard & Louise Hebbard
Steve & Nicky Fitzgerald
Antonio José Alfredo Spohr
Francioso family
The Maguire family
Robert Engels
Alan H.Y. Wong
Guido de Smet & Anita van Loo
James William Davey
Graham & Sally McDonald
Simon & Elly Moore
Scott O. Seydel
Sisley
Duncan Ross & Margaret Taylor
Horst Lotz
Michael Sell

Jeni & David Sieff
Luca Longaretti
Serge Sassonia
The Murphy family
Alex & Di Barrell
James & Trish Marshall & family
Mr. & Mrs. Rupert Horley & family
Peter & Jeff Williams
Jan & Elizabeth Nel
John Hurst Gallien & Shelby Webb Gallien
Mr. & Mrs. Chia Cheng Guan
Jane Ellen Gallien-Sanders & Stephen
  Goss Sanders
Bob Crisp
Amy Josephine Brennan
Alistair Ian McGlashan
Janine Bombardier & Sadok Besrour
Mike G. Lourens
Bill, Debbie, Drew & Wes Lipner
Jim, Linda, Elisabeth, Sara & John Tullis
Petra & Paul Betschart
John Carter Race
Insouth
Timothy C.M. Chia
Peter Zandan & family
Bill Lipner
Neena & Shrik Mehta

Christine & James Holden
Annette & Andrea Magni & family
Patricia Ann Toop
Claire & Mohan Mediratta
Steve Hall
Clive John West
Vicki & Nigel Colne
Jessica Kelly
Graham Bonham-Carter
Dr. Simon & Jane Chinchanwala
Foster & Sallie Bam
T.L. de Beer
Didier de Vos
Hugh Marshall & Julie Holl
Andy & Pat Ochse
Peter Stein
Nedcor Bank Ltd.
Kathleen & Robert Ridder
Geert & Els Verf
Sten Jessen
Mr. & Mrs. Kenneth Chia
Kunj & Devyani K. Trivedi
Suzanne Patricia Eloff
G. R. Thomson
Karen Edmondson
Craig Clucas
Boy & Liz Barrell

SPECIAL SUBSCRIBERS

John Ernest Abels
Robert Abendanon – Exatrade
Natalie Abratt
Douglas Adler & family
Mial Ainge
Mohalhil A.A.M. Al-Khalid & Rana Y.Y Al-Hamed
Amanpuri
Des & Ann Anderson
Dr. & Mrs. Donald Andress
Shelley & Brian Aronson
Jonathan G. Arthur
Linda Arthur
Grant & Sandy Ashfield
John & Margie Austin
Mrs. Rose Austin
N. C. Axelson
Krista Kay Ayers
Muffin & Kenji Balajardia
Alberto Ballerini
Carlo Ezio Ballerini
Foster & Sallie Bam
Alison & Paul Bannister
Ray Barlow
Denis Barnard
Malcolm & Peta Anne Basford
Coke & Paula Bayvel
Peter Hill Beard
Chris, Natalie, Bradley & Christyn Bedser
Div Beeb & family
Darryl G. Behrman
Archie & Glynis Bell
Suzanne Leza Benadie
Dovie Binder
Mark Binks
Dino Biscaro
Steen Bjerre
David Blumberg
Peter & Gillian Bode
Mr. & Mrs. Charles Bone
Amedeo & Carla Bove
John R. Bradshaw
John & Carol Brandtner
Dr. C. A. Brecher
M. H. Brodie
Carol & Christopher Browne
Mr. & Mrs. John Bruno
Ruth Bryant
Katja Buisson
Tatjana Buisson

Claudia & Jean Claude Buisson
Pat & Stella Butler
Wade Calenbourne & Lyndsay Tyler
Athol & Liz Campbell
Andrea & Maria Teresa Catanzano
Tim Caven
Mr. & Mrs. C. R. Cavendish-Davies
Mark Chaperone & family
Laurie & Rita Chiappini
Joggie & Linky Cilliers
Cowabunga Clarke
Gary Clarke & family
Tony Clarkson
Shona & David Clayton
Mr. & Mrs. Phil Clinton
Mr. & Mrs. John Clinton
Peter Clucas
Dorothy & Malcolm Coates
B. M. E. Coaton
Gavin & Thea Cohen
Richard Neil Colbourne
Robert & Hazel Conacher
Conservation Corporation Africa
Keith E. Cooke
Mr. & Mrs. Pace Cooper
Mr. & Mrs. Irby Cooper
Dr. Graham Coupland
Cindy Crawford
Peter & Verna Cronshaw
Ian Crooks
Michael Crowly
Des Cunningham
Kathleen I. Cunningham
Donald & Rosemary Currie
Dr. Raymond S. Damazo
Ron & Judy Davis
Bryce Davis
Lauren Davis
M. J. Davis
Patrick, Sue, Lane & Max Deale
Henry de Cazotte
Pete & Cheryl de Kock
Cheryl & Ajit de Fonseka
Troye de Jong
Nicola Delledonne
Solange de Penaranda
Peter & Dyanne de Vos
Kim & Debbie Densham
Miss Sabine Deville

Tracey Devonport
Sara Dewar
Helen Dewar
The Dolamores
Tim Driman
Kathleen du Bois
Graham Dumbrill
Bruce & Andi Durow
Mr. Brent Dyer
Justin Earle
Nikos E. Efthymiadis
Georg Erb – Swakopmund
Estée Lauder Cosmetics
Michael P. Ethelston
Gavin & Antoinette Faulds
Susan & Stuart Feinberg
Johan Ferreira
Joy & Geoff Fetting
David Foden
Robert Patrick Fordyce
Brian Stuart Forsgate – Hong Kong
J.M. Fourie
Francioso family
Trev & Jenny Franks
Russel, Bonnie & Gabriella Friedman
Richard Friedman
Adrian Frutiger
Malcolm Funston
Mary Belle Hurst Gallien
Jean Anne Gallien-Vaughn &
     David Jeffrey Vaughn
Conrad & Anne Garnett
Mr. & Mrs. Robert Gaston
Robert Gee
Dr. Herman Geldenhuys
Susan Gerry
Cristiana Giacinti
David & Marie Louise Gittens
Jon & Louise Glenton
Heather R. Goddard
Going Africa cc
Chelan & Sita Goonetilleke
P. W. Gordon-Grant
Ken Graham
Lindsay Gray
Paul & Helen Green
Rodney & Susan Green
Bob & Marlene Griffin
Joan & Peter Grossett

SPECIAL SUBSCRIBERS

Alayne Hadwick
Kelly Hagelthorn
Leonard Hall
Malou Hallström
Oria & Ian Douglas Hamilton
Katie & Ashleigh Hamilton-Fowle
Wayne, Lise, Donna & Rosalea Hanssen
H. William Harlan
Alex Harris
Sal & Nick Harris
Paul & Kathy Harris
Gillian Mary, Laura Jane & Geoffrey David Hart
Katja & Klaus Hartig
Gerrit & Lorraine Hartman
Stephen & Linda Heard
Ant & CC Hedley
Anton N. Heijstek
Simone Henselmans
Glynn & Anne Herbert
Mr. & Mrs. Tim Herndon
Dave & Margie Hidden
Jill Hill
Roy & Cheryl Hirst
Bethsy Holk
Mr. & Mrs. David Holt
Raymond Hoog
Martin John Horn
Nigel & Lesleé Hosking
John Huxter
Abraham Jaffe
Brenda James
Robin James
Ron & Jenny James & family
Roger & Sue Jankes
Leon & Marc Janks
David F. Jenkins
Johannesburg Public Library
Rupert Johnson – Exatrade
'Bones' & Jenny Jones
Paul Tudor Jones
G. P. Kemp
Dilip Khatau
Paul & Laurel Kinsley
Billy Kirstein
Thomas Klinger Lohr & family
David & Noleen Knott
Tom Koor
Philip & Michele Krawitz
Carl & Liesl Kriegisch

Lara Kriegisch
Keith & Germaine Krog
Anne-Marie & Martin Kubitschek
Peter Kuhnert
S. Kumaranayagam
Ilene Langton
Alden & Constace Lank
Jane & Martin Lawrence
R. M. Lawrie
Simon & Gail Laxton
Rusty Leach
Klaus & Pattie Lederer
Astrid & Michel Ledin
Samantha Lee
Dr. Donald E. Leisey
Nan & Don Lennard
Bruce "Banana" Lennox
Elmor & Doria Leo
Hillary Shannon Lewis Soma
Mr. & Mrs. Kent Lillie
George Longbotham
Gordon Lord – Exatrade
Helmut Lotti
Horst Lotz
Piet & Lynne Louw
Bridget & Roderick Lupton
Margie MacDuff
Muriel MacRobert
Main Industries (Pty) Limited
Daniele Malinverno
D.G. Martin
Nick Martin
Carlos Matos-Lopes
Rodney Mattheys & Kevin Gaffney
Donald & Joyce McCarten
Kathryn McCarten
Mike & Yolande McDonogh
Liz McGrath
Jim & Sharon McKelvey
Brian & Martha McMahon
Patrick C. McMahon
Michael E. McMahon
Axel S. Meinhold
David & Miriam Meltzer
Terry Meredith & Joy Taylor
Merison
I. P. D. Merriman
Ute Meyer
Edward Meyer

Daniel Michel
James & Laura Miller
Dr. Rob Milnes
David Mitchell
Dave & Carol Mommsen
Beatrice Monfanari & Urs Christen
Silvana Montorfano
Simon & Elly Moore
Milou Morlion
Norman E. Morris & Ann Marie Gustafsson
Rad & Heather Morrison
José-Oriol Mosso Goberna
P. R. Mulder
Neil Munro
Craig & Inge Murray
Dennis Murray
Namibrand Nature Reserve
Richard C. M. Napier
Katrin Neiman
Louise Holden Neville
Georgio Nicolli & family
James Barry Nisbet
Michael & Fiona Nixon
N.T.C. (Pty) Limited
Elsje O'Flaherty
K. Ochse
Gareth Ochse
Jay & Cherry Owen
Caroline Paget
Hans Pahle
Basil H. Pappin
Robert & Val Parker
Ross & Renée Parry-Davies
Andrew Paterson
Nigel Paul
Don & Lynn Payne
Val & Geoff Pearce
John & Jeannine Pearse
Lisa Pearse
Geoff & Jenny Peatling
Anne & Anthony Peepall
William & Betty Pendarvis
Martin & Eileen Penrose
Leesha Perera
John & Maureen Perkins
Bethany Jayne Ellison Perrett
Sylvie & Wolfgang Peter
Di Pheasant
Mel Piëst

SPECIAL SUBSCRIBERS

James Pollin
Silvia & Franco Postizzi
Jenny & Peter Price
Charles Priebatsch
Rob Purkiss
Sandy & Theo Rabie
Marcel Rast – Exatrade
Hugh & Jessica Rawdon
Lloyd Rennie
Nini Rennie-Vranyczany
Lynne & Philip Richardson
Giorgio Rizzi
Madeleine Robbertse
Judy Robertson
Alexandra & Eliane Roessingh
Rosmarin family
W. Ross
Byron Ross
Mark & Sally Rowand
Patricia Royle
Gaynor Allison Rupert
Sean & Carol Ryan
Stefano Salice
Trisha Salmon
Stanley S. Savage
Dato & Datin Samsudin
Savannah Tented Safari Lodge
Alan Sawyer
Lawrence & Linda Keen Scharer
Paul & Lorato Scherpenhuyzen
Barry & Diane Scott
Campbell E. L. Scott
Karl & Toni Seger
Albert W. Seifert
Scott O. Seydel
Phyllis & Bruce Seymour
Robert Seynaeve
Sudhir L. Shah
Janet & Perry Short
Jo & Pam Smith
Nick Smith

Lionel Paul Smith
Hans Smith & family
Martin Smullen
Mr. James T. Snyder
Mr. & Mrs. Donald R. Snyder
Nicki Spice
Andreas Spyron
Roger & Rosa Stacey
Adrian Stanbridge
June Stannard
Basil & Ines Stathoulis
Susan & Christian Stenderup
Helen L. Stewart
Chris & Belinda Steyn
K. M. S. Stimpson
Julia Stockham
Gary & Jill Strand
Jenny Street
Pieter & Pam Struik
Terri & Jolene Stupel
D. H. B. Sülter
James & Amanda Sunley
Johan & Elsabe Swart
Arnold Tanzer
Lorette Taylor
Ryan, Kestrel & Scott Taylor
Noel Havelock Tearle
Gavin Tennant
Mark Tennant
Katherine KTC Terry
Diane & Maurice Terry
Ian, Moira, Clyde & Lara Thomas
David & Anne Thompson
Charles Maurice Thompson
Elizabeth S. H. Thomson
Damian & Chrissie Timms
Dominique Tiphaine
Robert Bruce Todd
Gina Toh
Prashant & Shveta Trivedi
Mehul Trivedi

Jane Trotman
Tumbela Lodge
University of Pretoria
Russell Upneck
Nicolas Urbain
Catherine & Frans van Aart-Poels
Eric van Daalen
Dick & Liz van der Jagt
M. van der Mark
Kathy Lyn van der Merwe
Mart van der Westhuizen
Marco van Embden
M. & M. A. van Rijswijck
Henry & Margaret van Wyk
Johan van Wyk
Garnet & Joan Venn
Adré Venter
Jan & Winnie Venter
Andre Verhaag
Bruno, Gilles & Charlotte Verhulst
Reni von Schöning & Jan Troelsch
Anton von Well
Hannie Voorma
Johan Vosloo
Frazer Walker
Grant Wall
Craig & Majorie Walsh
A. R. Walwyn
Maureen "Gogs" Watson
Alan & Jane Weaving
Ron & Di Webb
George & Gene Webb
Bryan Christopher West
David Infield Whittome
Vicky & Julia Willmott
Molly Ann Wilson
Hilda & Jurgen Witt
Hans & Renata Wollny
Richard Grant Wood
Derek & Joan Wright
Fergus Wylie

REFERENCE

Bibliography

African Insect Life. S.H. Skaife. Struik Publishers. 1994.

Snakes and Other Reptiles of Southern Africa. Bill Branch Field Guide. Struik Publishers. Cape Town. 1996.

Blue Wildebeest Population Trends in the Kruger National Park and the effects of fencing, by I J Whyte & S C J Joubert. 1987.

Game and Gold. Memories of over 50 years in the Lydenburg District Transvaal. 1873 – 1925. Henry Glynn. The Dolman Printing Company Limited, London.

Game Ranger by Hannes Kloppers. Juta and Co. Ltd. Cape Town. About 1970.

Jock of the Bushveld by Sir Percy Fitzpatrick. Longmans, Green and Co. Ltd., London and Harlow. First printed 1907.

Kruger National Park Questions & Answers. Struik Publishers, Cape Town, 1992.

Long Walk to Freedom: The Autobiography of Nelson Mandela. Published by Macdonald Purnell in South Africa. 1994.

Mammals of Southern Africa. Chris and Tilde Stuart. Struik Publishers. 1996.

Memories of a Game Ranger by Harry Wolhuter. Wildlife Protection Society. 1948.

Naturalist by Edward O. Wilson published by Penguin Press, London. 1994.

Paradise under Pressure by Alan Mountain. Southern Book Publishers, Johannesburg.

Pennington's Butterflies of Southern Africa. Published by Struik Winchester, 1994.

Piet van Wyk's Field Guide to the Trees of the Kruger National Park. Struik, 1984.

Princess Alice, Countess of Athlone by Theo Aronson. Publishers: Cassell. London. 1981.

Standard Encyclopedia of Southern Africa. Volume 6. Nasou Limited. Cape Town. 1972.

Roberts' Birds of Southern Africa. Gordon Lindsay Maclean. John Voelcker Bird Book Fund. 1993.

Stories from the Karkloof Hills by Charles Scott Shaw. Shuter & Shooter, Pietermaritzburg. 1971.

South African Eden – The Kruger National Park by James Stevenson-Hamilton. Struik Publishers. Cape Town. 1993.

The Conservationists and the Killers by John Pringle. T.V. Bulpin & Books of Africa. 1982.

The Kaleidoscopic Transvaal by Carl Jeppe.

The Kruger National Park. A Social and Political History by Jane Carruthers. University of Natal Press. Pietermartizburg. 1995.

The Last Lion by William Manchester. Michael Joseph Ltd. 1983.

The Leopards of Londolozi. Magazine article by Alf Wannenburgh. Published 1983.

The Leopards of Londolozi by Lex Hes. Struik Publishers. Cape Town. 1991.

The South African Railways , General Manager, S.A. Railways. 1947.

The South-Eastern Transvaal Lowveld. Lowveld Regional Development Association, Barberton. 1954.

The Transvaal of Today by Alfred Aylward. 1928. William Blackwood & Sons, Edinburgh.

The Trees of the Kruger National Park. Piet van Wyk. Struik Publishers. 1990.

Transvaal Consolidated Land & Exploration Company Ltd. Annual reports 1920 – 1938.

Trees of Natal, Zululand & Transkei. Elsa Pooley. Natal Flora Publications Trust. 1994.

Wild Flowers of KwaZulu-Natal. Joan Walker. W.R. Walker Family Trust. 1996.

Wild Flowers of South Africa. Struik Publishers. Cape Town. 1993.

Unpublished manuscripts:

Sparta Game book 1942 – 1969 and *Sabi Sand Wildtuin* by Madeleine Varty. 1975.

Londolozi Game Reserve by John Varty.

Quotations

Title, *King Henry IV, Part II* by William Shakespeare. Chapter 1, *Some Reasons Why* by Robert Green Ingersoll; Chapters 2 and 5, *The Sappi Collection* by Peter Johnson and Creina Bond © 1983 with the kind permission of the authors; Chapter 3, *Unto this Last* by John Ruskin; Chapter 4, Gary Lawless from *First Sight of Land*, by permission of publisher and author, Blackberry Books, RRI, Box 228, Nobleboro, ME 04555; Chapter 6 & 7, *Regimen* and *Aphorisms* by Hippocrates, trans. by Chaucer; Chapter 8, *In the Neolithic Age* by Rudyard Kipling; Chapter 10, by John Ruskin; Chapter 11, King George V.

Photographic Reference

Lex Hes: dust jacket front cover, title pages (4), pages, 2, 3, 4, 15, 16, 19, 24, 25(3), 26(2), 30, 32, 38, 42, 43, 45(4), 48(2), 49, 50, 51(2), 53, 54, 56/57, 59, 61(2), 62(2), 65(2), 66(2), 68, 70, 71, 72/73, 80/81, 82, 83, 87(7), 89, 90(3), 91(2), 92, 93, 94(2), 96(3), 97, 98, 102, 103, 104(2), 105, 106(2), 107(2), 109(2), 110(2), 111(2), 112(2), 114, 115(2), 117, 118(2), 120/121, 122, 123, 124, 125(2), 127(5), 129, 130, 131(3), 143(3), 144, 147, 158(2), 162, 163(3), 166, 168, 170, 171(4), 172, 173, 174(2), 179, 180, 182(2), 183, 184, 185, 186, 187(2), 190, 191, 200, 201(3), 203, 204(5), 207(2), 209.

Peter Johnson (Corbis): book cover, pages 27, 40/41, 58, 84, 100/101, 150, 183, 186, 191, 198/199.

Richard du Toit: pages, 17, 19, 20, 30, 31, 46, 53, 65, 68, 69(2), 114, 116, 118, 132, 135, 137, 138, 146, 163, 164(2), 176/177, 183, 184, 186(2), 187, 194(2), 201, 204, 205, 208, 217.

Guy Stubbs: pages, 133, 165(2), 167(2), 172, 179(2), 202(2),

James Marshall: pages, 19, 113, 205.

Mike Myers: page 124.

G.P.L. du Plessis: page 126.

ABPL Photo Library: pages 12, 19, 34, 117, 127, 136, 150, 154(2), 159, 189(3), 191, 195.

JBP Photo Library: pages, 75, 128, 147, 187, 204(2),

Londolozi Productions: pages 140/141, 142, 144, 145, 148, 149(2), 151, 152, 153(3), 156, 157, 191, 193, 196, 203.

Conservation Corporation: pages 160/161, 168(2), 169(2), 174, 178, 181(2), 184, 188(2), 192(9), 193, 196(3).

Stephen Doig: Sketch of President Mandela with JV, Dave and Shan Varty.

Johan Hoekstra: Wildlife illustrations on dust jacket and on pages: 21, 39, 55, 79, 99, 119, 139, 159, 175, 197, 209.

All deep-etched marginal photographs: Johan Hoekstra and Molly Buchanan.